MAX notes®

Alice Walker's

The Color Purple

Text by
Christopher Hubert
(B.A., Bates College)
Department of English
Oryol Pedagogical University, Oryol, Russia

Illustrations by
Jerome Press

Research & Education Association
Visit our website at
www.rea.com

Research & Education Association
61 Ethel Road West
Piscataway, New Jersey 08854
E-mail: info@rea.com

MAXnotes® for
THE COLOR PURPLE

Year 2006 Printing

Printed in the United States of America

Library of Congress Control Number 00-112223

International Standard Book Number 0-87891-009-3

What **MAXnotes**® *Will Do for You*

This book is intended to help you absorb the essential contents and features of Alice Walker's *The Color Purple* and to help you gain a thorough understanding of the work. Our book has been designed to do this more quickly and effectively than any other study guide.

For best results, this **MAXnotes** book should be used as a companion to the actual work, not instead of it. The interaction between the two will greatly benefit you.

To help you in your studies, this book presents the most up-to-date interpretations of every section of the actual work, followed by questions and fully explained answers that will enable you to analyze the material critically. The questions also will help you to test your understanding of the work and will prepare you for discussions and exams.

Meaningful illustrations are included to further enhance your understanding and enjoyment of the literary work. The illustrations are designed to place you into the mood and spirit of the work's settings.

This **MAXnotes** book analyzes and summarizes each section as you go along, with discussions of the characters and explanations of the plot. A biography of the author and examination of the work's historical context will help you put this literary piece into the proper framework of what is taking place.

The use of this study guide will save you the hours of preparation time that would ordinarily be required to arrive at a complete grasp of this work of literature. You will be well prepared for classroom discussions, homework, and exams. The guidelines that are included for writing papers and reports on various topics will prepare you for any added work that may be assigned.

The **MAXnotes** will take your grades "to the max."

Larry B. Kling
Chief Editor

Contents

Each Letter includes List of Characters, Summary, Analysis, Study Questions and Answers, and Suggested Essay Topics.

MAXnotes® are simply the best – but don't just take our word for it...

"... I have told every bookstore in the area to carry your MAXnotes. They are the only notes I recommend to my students. There is no comparison between MAXnotes and all other notes ..."
– *High School Teacher & Reading Specialist,*
Arlington High School, Arlington, MA

"... I discovered the MAXnotes when a friend loaned me her copy of the *MAXnotes for Romeo and Juliet*. The book really helped me understand the story. Please send me a list of stores in my area that carry the MAXnotes. I would like to use more of them ..."
– *Student, San Marino, CA*

A Glance at Some of the Characters

Celie

Mr.___(Albert)

Nettie

Shug Avery

Harpo

Sofia Butler

Alphonso

Reverend Samuel

SECTION ONE

Introduction

The Life and Work of Alice Walker

Alice Walker is one of the most famous and beloved writers of our time, and this is largely due to the novel *The Color Purple*. Born on February 9, 1944, Walker was the youngest of eight children and the daughter of sharecroppers. She was always a precocious child, but after being blinded in one eye at age eight in an accident with a BB gun, Walker became more insecure and withdrawn. Walker has always given credit to her mother for encouraging her to make something of herself; her father and four of her five brothers failed to give her a positive male role model. She was especially influenced by her father's brutality, which served as a model for Mr.____ in *The Color Purple*. She reconciled her feelings with her father once she understood the difficult life he had led and the abuse that he himself experienced (his mother was murdered coming out of church).

Walker entered Spelman College on a scholarship in 1961. Although Spelman was a mainstream college with a moderate point of view, Walker took part in civil rights demonstrations. In 1964, she transferred to Sarah Lawrence College. It was during this time that she would suffer a personal crisis that would deeply affect her life. After a trip to Africa, Walker returned to America pregnant, which isolated her from her family and threw her into a deep depression. Even though her father had expected his sons to experiment with sex, he had warned his daughters not to become pregnant. (Winchell, 28). Walker contemplated suicide, and even slept with a razor blade under her pillow, but "...a friend saved her life by giving her the phone number of an abortionist" (Winchell, 9). She recorded her experiences during this phase of her life in a book of poems, which became her first published collection.

Walker became a literary scholar after her graduation, but her work was impeded by "the blind spot" that she felt was in the education that she had received. Walker was fascinated by female writers such as Flannery O'Connor but eventually became frustrated by the lack of black women writers in the curriculum of colleges. Even when she did find black writers being taught, only prominent male writers such as Richard Wright and Langston Hughes were ever discussed. Walker eventually "discovered" the works of Zora Neale Hurston, a writer in the mid-twentieth century whose apolitical work was shunned in favor of authors such as Wright. Hurston became the biggest influence on her literary career and life. Walker eventually edited a collection of Hurston works and is largely responsible for her posthumous popularity. Hurston is best known for her 1937 novel *Their Eyes Were Watching God*, which has become a classic in twentieth century American literature.

Like Hurston, Alice Walker's lifestyle has been controversial and chaotic. She married the white civil rights attorney Melvyn Leventhal in 1968 but divorced in 1976. Unlike Hurston, Walker has been fiercely political; she has been a prominent lesbian and feminist, and her political views have been made the focus of her novels. Her first novels, *The Third Life of Grange Copeland* and *Meridian*, both dealt with violence towards black women by black males. *The Color Purple* also shared many of these themes. *Possessing the Secret of Joy* was a 1992 novel that dealt with female circumcision, which is used in some African rituals. Critics of Walker have stated that she has portrayed black men as cruel in her works, which has sustained stereotypes of black male violence.

The Color Purple was Walker's third novel, written in 1982. Her novel received the Pulitzer Prize for literature and an American Book Award. A film was made in 1985, which was critically acclaimed despite the fact that the screenplay departs dramatically from the novel. The most obvious differences are the exclusion of Nettie as a central character, and the almost complete removal of the subplot of Nettie, Corrine, and Samuel in Africa. The lesbian relationship between Shug and Celie is toned down as well, although the violence towards Celie seems as chilling in the movie as it is in the novel. The movie went on to receive 11 Academy Award nominations. In addition to her other novels, two of which, *The Temple of My Familiar* and *Possessing the Secret of Joy*, form a loose trilogy with *The Color Purple*, Walker has published two collections of short stories, poems, and political essays.

For more information on Alice Walker and her works, read the excellent biography by Donna Haisley Winchell (1992). Two other recommended books concerning black female writers are *The Common Bond*, a collection of essays edited by Lillie P. Howard, and *Black Women Novelists*, by Barbara Christian.

Historical Background

Alice Walker was active in the social events in her time, speaking out against injustice during civil rights demonstrations in the 1960s. Her feminism and activism in women's issues reflect the novels of Zora Neale Hurston, a writer in the 1930s. Alice Walker sets *The Color Purple* during the same time period as Hurston's novel *Their Eyes Were Watching God*. Hurston's then contemporary novel drew criticism for its portrayal of black men as abusive. Hurston was criticized by her black peers as well; it was believed that by commenting upon the unequal relationships between black men and women, Hurston diverted attention from the social inequality of blacks and whites. The novel concerns the efforts of Janie Crawford to escape the oppressiveness of her first two husbands. When Janie finally does find love, it is with a man 18 years her junior. Essayists writing about *The Common Bond* have commented that *The Color Purple* is a reworking of Hurston's plot with added elements such as lesbianism and the success of women outside the typical framework of marriage.

It is impossible to fully understand the ideas and plots of Alice Walker without first reading the works of Zora Neale Hurston, particularly *Their Eyes Were Watching God* and her autobiography, *Dust Tracks on a Road*. One gains valuable insight by reading these works. Walker, like Hurston, was very interested in African folklore, particularly the religious themes of the presence of God within nature. This theme is used very effectively in *The Color Purple*. Like Hurston, Walker does touch upon the social issues of 1930s

America, but focuses upon the broader picture of how men and women relate with each other today. Walker perhaps focuses more upon the relationships between men and women, rather than white and black, which has caused her to be the target of critics, much as Hurston was a target in her day. Walker has managed to comment on social issues while focusing upon character development in her works. *The Color Purple* is unquestionably a novel with a social message, but the larger issues in it concern a woman's personal struggle for freedom, and how she accomplishes this in a society where women are looked upon as inferior.

Master List of Characters

Celie—*The protagonist of* The Color Purple. *She is 14 at the beginning of the novel.*

Nettie—*Celie's younger sister.*

Mr. ____ (Albert)—*A local farmer who wants to marry Nettie, but is talked into marrying Celie by Alphonso.*

Shug Avery—*A nightclub singer who has had an ongoing relationship with Mr.____ despite his marriages.*

Harpo—*The eldest son of Mr.____ from a previous marriage. He is 12 years old when Celie and Mr.____ marry.*

Sofia Butler—*Harpo's independent wife.*

Celie's father (Alphonso) and mother—*Alphonso is the owner of a farm and store; his first wife dies at the beginning of the novel.*

May Ellen—*Alphonso's second wife.*

Olivia—*The daughter of Celie and Alphonso, she is given to Samuel and Corrine at birth.*

Adam—*The son of Celie and Alphonso, he is given to Samuel and Corrine at birth.*

Samuel (The Reverend Mr.____)—*The local reverend, and husband to Corrine.*

Corrine—*Wife to Samuel, she is a missionary preparing to leave for Africa.*

Squeak (Mary Agnes)—*Harpo's girlfriend.*

Old Mr.____—*Mr.____'s father and landlord to Mr.____'s farm.*

Kate and Carrie—*Mr.____'s sisters.*

Tobias—*Mr.____'s brother.*

Odessa and Jack—*Sofia's sister and brother-in-law, they also take care of Sofia's children.*

The Mayor and Miss Millie—*The couple who take Sofia as their maid after she is arrested.*

Eleanor Jane and Billy—*The daughter and son of Miss Millie and the Mayor.*

Grady—*Shug's husband, a marijuana grower and mechanic from Nashville.*

Tashi—*A young African girl from the Olinka tribe.*

Tashi's mother (Catherine) and father—*Members of the Olinka tribe.*

Joseph—*The guide of the missionaries.*

Henry Buster Broadnax—*Sofia's well-built boyfriend.*

Swain—*Harpo's friend and guitar player at the local nightclub.*

Daisy—*Alphonso's third wife.*

Jolentha (Suzie Q)—*The little daughter of Squeak and Harpo.*

Henrietta—*The little daughter of Sofia.*

Jerene and Darlene—*Twins who help Celie with her sewing. Darlene becomes interested in teaching Celie how to speak.*

Doris Baines—*An eccentric, successful author and missionary from England.*

Harold—*A small African child and the adopted grandson of Doris Baines.*

Althea and Theodosia—*Samuel's aunt and Corrine's aunt, respectively, they spent their lives together working as missionaries.*

Edward DuBoyce—*A young Harvard scholar.*

Germaine—*A young musician who becomes involved with Shug.*

Stanley Earl and Reynolds Stanley—*Eleanor Jane's husband and son.*

Summary of the Novel

The novel focuses upon the growth and development of a girl named Celie. Raped at 14 by her own father and then forced into a marriage with a cruel older man, Celie learns to be quiet and submissive. The person she cares most about, her sister Nettie, is forced out of her own home and kicked out of Celie's home by her husband, Mr.____. Mr.____ had married Celie so that she could take care of his children and work for him, since he is already in love with Shug Avery.

When Shug Avery falls ill, Mr.____ keeps her at his home. Thanks to Celie's care, Shug is able to recover and the two women begin a friendship. Over time, Celie learns to stand up for herself and gain self-respect. Celie also learns how to love, as the two women become lovers as well as friends. Shug promises Celie that she will stay and protect her from the abuse of Mr.____.

Nettie, meanwhile, finds refuge at the home of Samuel, the local reverend, and his wife, Corrine. Corrine and Samuel have two adopted children, Adam and Olivia. Celie is actually the mother of these children; they were taken from her by her father before she married Mr.____. Eventually the entire family, including Nettie, is sent to Africa for work as missionaries. They attempt to teach African children about Christianity. Nettie becomes involved in the struggle to educate a young African girl, Tashi, despite the wishes of her father, who believes that women should follow the custom of striving to become good wives. Nettie also enters a conflict with Corrine, who believes that Adam and Olivia are the result of an affair Nettie had with Samuel. Corrine is convinced that this is what happened because the children resemble Nettie so closely.

Nettie finally tells Samuel and Corrine that Celie is the children's original mother, but by now Corrine doesn't believe anything she says. When Corrine falls ill with a fever and comes close to death, Nettie becomes more desperate to make her believe the truth. Finally, Corrine remembers an early meeting that she had with Celie and dies understanding that Nettie had never had a relationship with Samuel. As the years pass, however, Nettie and Samuel fall in love and marry. Eventually, the missionaries are unable to save the Olinka tribe, whose land has been taken by developers. They plan to return to America and rescue Celie from her unhappy marriage. Nettie chronicles her adventures in Africa by writing letters to Celie twice a year. These letters, however, are taken by Mr.____ and hidden from Celie, who believes her sister is gone forever.

When Celie, with Shug's help, finds out that Mr.____ has been hiding these letters, she makes a stand and leaves Mr.____'s house. She learns how to live life on her own and how to take care of others, all the while waiting for Nettie. After her departure from Mr.____'s farm, Mr.____ and his son Harpo learn to be kinder to each other and to others. Celie enjoys a life of independence and eventually accepts and reconciles with the people who have treated her cruelly. The climax of the novel occurs when Nettie returns with Samuel, Olivia, Adam and Tashi, who has married Adam. After a tearful reunion, Celie, after all her suffering, is the happiest she has ever felt in her life.

The unique structure of the novel should be noted. Walker uses first-person narration, that is, the action of the novel is written through the eyes of the character Celie.

Celie's narration takes place in the form of letters, first to God, then to her sister Nettie. Nettie's adventures are told through her point of view, through letters written to Celie. Therefore, the plot of the text is actually two separate stories, loosely connected through Celie's relationship with Nettie. Celie and Nettie comment on their shared experiences, such as Celie's relationship with Mr.____ and the discovery of Celie's children, allowing the reader to fill in the gaps left by only one perspective in narration.

Estimated Reading Time

The 295-page novel is divided into 90 "letters," most of which are between one and two pages long. For the sake of convenience, the study guide is broken into 21 sections, based upon logical pauses in the action of the novel. Readers should be able to complete the novel in 10-12 hours.

The Color Purple

Letters 1–9

New Characters:

Celie: *a 14-year-old girl who is the protagonist of* The Color Purple

Alphonso and his wife: *Celie's mother and father*

Nettie: *Celie's younger sister*

Mr. ____: *a local farmer who wants to marry Nettie, but ends up marrying Celie*

May Ellen: *Alphonso's second wife*

Harpo: *the 12-year-old son of Mr.____ from a previous marriage*

Summary

    The novel begins with a letter to God, written by Celie, a young girl who has "always been a good girl." Celie starts writing to God when she is 14, saying that she wants to know "what is happening to me." One day last spring, she noticed her parents fighting. Her father wants to make love, but her mother refuses because she is too sick from recently giving birth. They are still arguing a week later. When her mother leaves the house in order to visit her sister, who is a doctor, Celie's father quickly catches Celie and rapes her, telling her that she is "gonna do what your Mammy wouldn't." The father also warns her that she "better...git used to it." Celie, however, "don't never git used to it," and becomes pregnant. Soon after she gives birth to her child, a little girl, her mother dies. When Celie is sleeping, her father takes her child away, and does it again when Celie gives birth a second time, to a little boy.

After Celie's mother dies, her father starts to look at Celie's younger sister, Nettie. Celie promises to protect Nettie until her father marries again, and one time even offers herself to her father when he wants to take Nettie. Even though her father marries another young girl, Nettie then finds herself being examined by Mr.____, who is as old as their father and a widower. Mr.____ soon asks their father for Nettie's hand in marriage but he rejects the proposal and offers him Celie instead. Mr.____ hadn't even considered marrying Celie, but decides to marry her because she is a hard worker and his "poor little ones could sure use a mother." While Mr.____ and their father discuss his marriage to Celie, Celie finds out that Mr.____'s last wife was murdered and that he has had an ongoing affair with Shug Avery, a local singer. After a few months, Mr.____ decides to marry Celie, who is about 20 years old.

Celie spends her wedding day "running from the oldest boy" of Mr.____. Harpo, 12 years old, attacks Celie with a rock as soon as she gets to Mr.____'s home. She immediately finds that her life is working and taking care of four ungrateful children. Celie spends her time thinking about Nettie, and wondering "if she safe." When she has sex with Mr.____, she thinks about Shug Avery, knowing that "what he doing to me he done to Shug Avery and maybe she like it." Although she knows that she is in an unpleasant situation, Celie refuses to cry.

Analysis

The opening letters of this novel introduce us to Celie, a young girl who endures what seems to be nothing but abuse and betrayal. Her reasons for writing to God are clear. "You better not never tell nobody but God. It'll kill your mammy," is what Celie's father says to her before he rapes her. Celie is left without a mother she can confide in and with a father who abuses her. Living in a hopeless situation, she looks to God for guidance and assistance. She grows up in a family that demands work from her and gives her nothing but pain in return.

We see that Celie is left to survive without support or love from her parents, who are the people expected to provide the child with security and love. Celie does not have the love of the family, the type of love that most of us take for granted. As a result, the world in which Celie lives seems very cruel to the reader. What is even more repugnant is the rape of Celie by her father; a heinous crime to begin with, the rape here is also symbolic. Just as the crime violates the woman and takes away her security and trust, Celie loses not only her trust of society but also her trust of her own family. She cannot even consider herself safe in the one place where she should be able to depend on it. Celie's trust in the family unit is betrayed, yet her father still relies on her loyalty to protect him from her mother, who confronts Celie about her pregnancy. The threat at the beginning of the book shifts the responsibility of keeping the secret to Celie. She feels shame, although it is her father who has committed the crime.

Walker uses these opening pages to illustrate the inequitable treatment of men and women in society. Celie is young and especially vulnerable, since the abuser is her father and already has a position of power over her. Celie, like the other women in these opening pages, is at the mercy of the men who have the power in this society. This idea will be a theme that runs through the novel. To her father, and to the other men of this town, women are disposable and forgettable units, only useful for providing themselves with pleasure. Celie's father uses his daughter to replace her mother, who is too hurt from childbirth to have intercourse. When Celie becomes older, her father replaces her deceased mother with another young girl, and then starts to pursue Nettie when his new wife becomes sick. To this man, the women of *The Color Purple* are interchangeable, used for sex and then for work.

Celie is also isolated by the fact that she is not allowed to have even a stereotypically female role in this family. When she gives birth to two children, they are taken away, denying Celie her rightful role as a mother. (This role is symbolized by the wasted milk "running down" Celie's body.) Her work is wasted on her brothers

and sisters, and later on Mr.____'s children, who are unapprecia-
tive and unwilling to help her with the enormous responsibility.
This effort is also ignored by her father, and her husband, who see
it as women's work and therefore also dismissable. Celie's wasted
efforts are the typical rewards for women in the novel; they receive
punishment for doing nothing and are ignored even when they are
working well. Celie's work is wasted because it is considered un-
important; she takes care of the children, but not within a nurtur-
ing relationship. She receives no love in return, which makes her
work pointless.

The situation concerning Mr.____'s last wife illustrates the
absurdity of women's roles in this society. Celie's father complains
that Mr.____'s wife caused a scandal by being murdered by a jealous boyfriend. The crime of having a lover is more evil to the men
in this society than a man killing a woman. This illustrates the
struggle that seems almost impossible for Celie to win.

Celie's one ally in this enormous struggle is Nettie, who attempts to teach her so that they might both escape from this cruel
place. However, Celie's bravery is taken away by her need for security and her desire to protect Nettie. As Nettie becomes older, Celie
sees that she is starting to be victimized by her abusive father as
well. Celie promises to protect her, but this is unrealistic—she could
hardly protect herself from this constant onslaught. She tries to
protect Nettie by offering herself as the victim to her father, and
then by marrying Mr.____. This act of self-sacrifice is extremely
brave, but Celie has numbed herself to the enormity of the abuse,
and therefore sees this act as natural.

The second way she tries to protect Nettie is "with God help."
This is about as effective for Nettie as it was for Celie.

Walker will use the image of the church throughout the novel
to contradict the hope that Celie gets from God. We learn that Celie
is slapped because her father "say I winked at a boy in church."
Mr.____'s previous wife was killed as she was stepping out of church.
This church is unable to protect women who look to God to deliver
them from the abuse they endure. Walker implies through the use
of this image that Celie's letters, and wishes, fall on deaf ears.

Her marriage to Mr.____ is by no means salvation for Celie.
Her new role as a wife is not respected by anyone; Mr.____ only

marries her after hearing that she is a good worker, and even then asks about the cow that Celie's father is willing to give him. When she is introduced to the children as their new mother, Harpo, the eldest child, hits her with a rock. Her role as a mother is also not accepted by the children, who cry and complain when she tends them. She is not loved by Mr.____, as evidenced by their sexual relationship. She thinks about Shug Avery, who becomes an ideal figure for her due to her beauty and her ability to enjoy making love with Mr.____. She takes comfort from her situation by worrying about Nettie, and concerning herself over her sister's safety.

Celie has proven in the novel's introduction that she is a survivor, but has survived only by numbing herself to both the pleasure and pain she could receive from life.

Study Questions

1. Who is Lucious?
2. What is Celie's answer when her mother asks her "Whose child is it"?
3. What does Celie think happened to her second child?
4. How old is Celie's new mother?
5. How did Mr.____'s previous wife die?
6. Why is Celie beaten by her father after she goes to church?
7. How many children does Mr.____ have?
8. Why does Celie's father reject Mr.____'s request to marry Nettie?
9. According to Celie's father, why will Celie be a better wife to Mr.____ than Nettie?
10. How long does it take for Mr.____ to decide to marry Celie?

Answers

1. Lucious is Celie's newborn brother.
2. Celie says that the child is God's.
3. Celie thinks that her father killed her first child, but believes that he sold her second child.

4. Celie's father marries a woman who is as old as Celie.

5. Supposedly, Mr.____'s previous wife was shot by her boy-friend when she left church.

6. Her father hits her because he thinks that she winked at a boy in church.

7. Mr.____ says he has three children, but Celie discovers that he actually has four children.

8. Nettie's father thinks Nettie is too young for a man like Mr.____. He has heard the rumors about the death of Mr.____'s previous wife and his relationship with Shug Avery. He also has made plans for Nettie to become a schoolteacher.

9. Celie is not as pretty as Nettie, "but she ain't no stranger to hard work," according to her father. He also says that "God done fixed her," meaning that Mr.____ can still do whatever he wants without worrying about interference from Celie.

10. Three months pass before Mr.____ decides to marry Celie.

Suggested Essay Topics

1. How come we do not know Mr.____'s last name? How does this symbolize the behavior of men in this society?

2. Look at the symbols of education in this section (the books, Miss Beasley...). How are they connected with the sisters' desire for a better life?

Letters 10–12

New Characters:

Olivia: *Celie's daughter, taken from Celie at birth*

The Reverend Mr.____ (Samuel): *Olivia's adopted father and hus-band to Corrine*

Corrine: *Olivia's adopted mother*

Kate and Carrie: *Mr.____'s sisters*

Summary

While Celie is at the dry goods store with Mr.____, she sees her daughter walking with Corrine. She begins to talk with Corrine and finds her to be a friendly and kind woman. When Corrine's husband is late picking them up, Celie offers a ride to her and Olivia. They are ready to accept, but the reverend comes by and whisks them away. Corrine tells Celie a joke as they leave, and Mr.____ wants to know why Celie is so happy as he comes out of the store.

Nettie moves in with Mr.____ and Celie after she runs away from home. Mr.____ still has a crush on Nettie, and spends most of his time complimenting her. This makes Nettie uncomfortable, and she keeps as far from him and as close to Celie as possible. After it becomes clear to Mr.____ that Nettie has no interest in him, he tells Celie that Nettie has to leave the next day. Celie tells Nettie to go to the reverend's house and ask for his wife, since she is "the only woman [she has] ever seen with money." Nettie leaves but begs Celie to fight the unfair treatment she receives from Mr.____ and his children. Celie tells Nettie to write her, but she never hears from Nettie again.

This is repeated when Kate and Carrie come to visit. They joke with Celie about Mr.____'s previous wife, Annie Julia, and compliment her cooking. A few days later, Kate returns by herself, and badgers her brother into buying a dress for Celie. However, when Kate tells Harpo to do some housework on his own, Harpo complains to his father. Mr.____ kicks his sister out of the house, and Kate, with tears in her eyes, tells Celie that she can't help anymore. Kate also begs Celie to fight for herself. Celie wonders how she can fight when Nettie fought her own family and had to run away. Celie knows she's not happy, but at least she is alive.

Analysis

Once Celie is married, she resigns herself to a life that is at best boring and uneventful and usually calls for work from dawn to dusk. After Walker shows us a woman at the mercy of men and a society which caters to men, she introduces elements of hope that are more effective than Celie's reliance on the church and God. These elements are embodied in the people Celie meets in this section of the novel.

Celie's first shock comes when she meets her own daughter, whom she feared was killed by her father. This moment is bittersweet, of course, because her daughter is now the foster child of the reverend and his wife. While the reverend's wife is a pleasant woman, her connection to the church is a symbol of the distance that Celie feels between herself and God. We can tell that the reverend's wife does not fully understand the society in which she lives; her comments on Mr.____ and his attractiveness indicate how withdrawn she is from the rest of the community. She only witnesses the town from inside the church, and never sees the violence that occurs after everyone goes home. Celie feels poor because she can sense her distance from the woman. At the same time, she is overjoyed that her daughter is in this family; Celie feels that Olivia is protected by her new mother. This protection is symbolized by the dress that the reverend's wife plans to make. When Celie and the reverend's wife trade jokes, the distance between Celie and God is temporarily closed. Celie is able to laugh for the first time in a long time, a moment that is quickly brought to an end by Mr.____'s return.

This contact is a definite contrast to her isolation in the previous section. The arrival of Nettie proves that Celie has other options in life than simply to agree to the wishes of Mr.____ and his ungrateful family. Kate also tries to protect Celie by making her a dress (the same symbol of protection that Olivia receives from her new mother) and by fighting back for Celie when she doesn't have the nerve to do it for herself. However, Mr.____ exhibits his ability to control Celie by simply removing these people from her life. Even when Kate manages to buy Celie a dress, Mr.____ exhibits control over what color of dress is chosen. Celie wants a purple dress, but cannot find one. Her second choice is red, but she chooses blue because she is afraid Mr.____ won't want to pay for red. Kate and Nettie leave, urging Celie to fight for herself and hoping that their examples have given to Celie enough strength to continue the struggle. Although Kate and Nettie are hurt by Celie's refusal to fight, they do not understand that she feels obligated by her loyalty to her marriage. While she doesn't feel any love for Mr.____, she has "always been a good girl," and still feels a need to do as she is told.

Kate's and Nettie's departures also give Celie the idea that it is futile to fight. Instead of looking at their independence as triumphant, she is afraid of their disappearance from her world. Celie says "I don't fight, I stay where I'm told. But I'm alive," implying that Kate and Nettie are both gone forever. Celie is in awe of the power of Mr.____ and his ability to get rid of people, so she is content to be alive. Her life, however, isn't a source of pleasure to her. Life means to her, above all, security, even though she is still abused at the hands of Mr.____ and by the wishes of his children. Ironically, she wishes to Nettie that she was buried so she wouldn't have to work. Ultimately, her fear of being alone and unprotected is greater than her wish to be free of Mr.____'s family. She still claims that "long as I can spell G-o-d I got somebody along," but this claim seems hollow given her unhappiness and her refusal to change her situation.

Study Questions

1. How does Celie know that it is her daughter at the store?

2. What is Olivia's foster mother buying at the general store, and why?

3. How old is Olivia now?

4. Why does Nettie show up at Mr.____'s farm?

5. Why does Celie start to feel good about herself?

6. How does Celie react to Nettie's concern about leaving her alone with Mr.____?

7. Why do Mr.____'s sisters begin to gossip, even though "it not nice to speak ill of the dead"?

8. How does Celie compare with Mr.____'s previous wife, according to Kate and Carrie?

9. What color does Celie want for her dress, and what color does she end up buying?

10. Why does Harpo refuse at first when Kate asks him to bring in a bucket of water?

Answers

1. The little girl has Celie's eyes.

2. Olivia's foster mother is buying some fabric and thread so that she can make dresses for herself and her daughter.

3. Olivia will be seven in November.

4. Nettie couldn't take living at home with Pa and might try to find help for the smaller children.

5. Nettie passes on all the compliments that she receives from Mr.____ to Celie.

6. Celie is philosophical, saying that God is still with her.

7. Even though they gossip about Annie Julia, Mr.____'s last wife, they insist that it is still the truth.

8. Celie is a much better housekeeper than Annie Julia ever was, according to Kate and Carrie. Furthermore, she takes care of the children and cooks very well. Kate and Carrie both consider Mr.____ to be a bit ungrateful to have such a good wife and not appreciate her.

9. Celie wants a purple dress, but can't find any purple fabric. She settles for a blue dress.

10. Harpo tells Kate that fetching water is "women work."

Suggested Essay Topics

1. Examine the mannerisms of the reverend's wife and compare her to Celie. What do you think makes her more confident than Celie? What does she have that Celie does not?

2. What insight do we get from Mr.____'s character after seeing him attempt to flirt with Nettie?

Letters 13-18

New Character:

Sofia Butler: *Harpo's new wife*

Summary

Harpo starts to ask questions about Mr.____'s marriage and confesses to Celie that he is in love. Harpo met a girl in church and even though they haven't even spoke to one another, he already plans to marry her. Meanwhile, Mr.____ becomes excited when Shug Avery comes to town to play in a nightclub. He fixes himself up in a way that he has never done for Celie. He tries to keep it from her, but Celie already knows. She wishes she could go and meet the woman she has pictured in her mind for so long. Mr.____ is gone for the weekend, and when he finally returns, he acts so strangely that Celie becomes even more curious about Shug. Even though she has "a million question to ast" about Shug, she is unable to get any answers.

Harpo's relationship with the girl becomes real, and Harpo confesses to Celie that the girl, Sofia Butler, is pregnant. Harpo has already met Sofia's father, and did not receive a blessing from him, on account of the scandal caused by his mother. Harpo then takes Sofia to meet his own father. Mr.____ looks at Sofia and refuses to give her permission to marry Harpo because he believes his son is young and limited and she could be tricking him into marrying her. Sofia laughs at this and says that she doesn't need Harpo or Mr.____'s property. Sofia moves to her sister's house and tells Harpo that she will be waiting for him when he is ready. Harpo, unable to convince his father, gets married in secret and then brings Sofia and their new baby home. Harpo and Sofia move into the shed behind Mr.____'s house and Mr.____ gives his son some money for working at the farm.

Analysis

Up to this point in the novel, the male characters have been represented by the cruel and hateful Mr.____ and by Celie's and

Nettie's father. As Harpo becomes older, a new example of male behavior is established. Harpo's questions about Mr.____ and his treatment of Celie show that he is ignorant of male roles save the one his father uses. Mr.____ tells Harpo that he beats Celie because she is his wife, and expects him to understand that it is normal for husbands to abuse their wives. However, when Harpo is in love, his feelings contradict the callous attitude that Mr.____ shows for Celie. Harpo is left without true understanding of a relationship, and turns to Celie for help.

This lack of understanding is even harder for Harpo when he is rejected by Sofia's father. Sofia's father specifically rejects Harpo because of the scandal in which his mother is involved. His mother's murder was the result of an ongoing affair; her lover killed her because he wanted her dead before she returned to her husband. The values of society place the blame upon the wife; wives are beaten because they are "stubborn," and Annie Julia's lover's role in the affair and subsequent murder is overlooked. In this society, it is not so unusual that men cheat on their wives, but wives who cheat apparently deserve to be killed. The bond between mother and child allows Harpo to look at this situation from a different perspective. When he complains to Celie that "it not her fault somebody kill her," he is making a point that Celie knew all along. For a male, however, this is a significant statement. It contradicts the values with which he was brought up.

Even Mr.____ displays true emotion and character in this section, although it is Shug Avery's appearance that brings about this emotion. His primping and preening in preparation for his visit with Shug amuses Celie because she has never experienced such behavior from him. Celie becomes even more fascinated by Shug because she is able to provoke this reaction out of Mr.____ without even seeing him. The effect is only heightened when Mr.____ returns and is too tired and morose to do anything abusive to Celie. This section employs foreshadowing for the eventual meeting between Shug and Celie.

The introduction of Sofia Butler also shows the effect that women can have upon men. Sofia is the first woman in this novel to successfully rebuke Mr.____'s attempt to control his environment. Furthermore, her presence inspires Harpo to stand up to his

father, something which we never would have expected him to do by himself. This strong female character is also an inspiration to Celie, and will provide her with a role model in the future.

The key to Sofia's strength is the support she receives from her other family members, especially her sisters. After the baby is born, Harpo and Sofia marry, and three sisters come to assist her in the marriage. This support is what Sofia had counted on when she stood up to Mr.____. Mr.____ responds to Sofia's independence by focusing upon Harpo and insisting that he assert his position in the marriage. Mr.____ does this by teasing him after he sees that Harpo is dutiful to Sofia and that she has the upper hand.

All the events of this section serve to draw away some of the attention from Celie. Celie is a passive observer in these events, and as an observer, shows that she is capable of good wisdom and judgment. She plays the role of confidante for the first time, to Harpo and Mr.____. She is a bit surprised by this new attention, especially when Mr.____ asks for her opinion. The new conflict between Harpo and Mr.____ also introduces some parity to this novel, and permits Celie to have a broader perspective. She says with a hint of happiness that "Harpo no better at fighting his daddy back than me." She doesn't feel any particular attachment to Harpo, so it doesn't hurt her to see him fight with Mr.____. She no longer feels as if she is the only person in the world who is abused, but now, she does nothing about it except allow herself to gloat.

Study Questions

1. What is the reason that Mr.____ gives Harpo for beating his wife?

2. How old is Harpo when he falls in love, and how old is the girl with whom he falls in love?

3. How does Celie know that Shug Avery is going to play at the Lucky Star?

4. Why does Celie want to go to the club?

5. Why does Celie follow Mr.____ back from the cotton fields?

6. Describe Harpo's recurring nightmare.

7. What does Sofia ask Celie for?

8. Where do Sofia and Harpo eventually marry?

9. Why does Mr.____ start to pay Harpo wages for working?

10. What does Mr.____ mean when he says to Harpo, "I see now she going to switch the traces on you"?

Answers

1. Mr.____ says that he beats her because she is his wife and "she stubborn."

2. Harpo is 17, and the girl he is in love with is 15.

3. Celie finds an advertisement for the club.

4. Celie wants "to lay eyes on her."

5. Celie thinks that Mr.____ is sick, when he is still not over his weekend with Shug Avery.

6. Harpo dreams that he is a witness to his mother's murder, and ends up cradling his dead mother in his arms.

7. Sofia asks Celie for a glass of water.

8. Sofia and Harpo marry at Sofia's sister's house.

9. Mr.____ thinks that wages will encourage Harpo to work harder.

10. Mr.____ means that Sofia is treating Harpo like he is a work-horse. It also implies that Harpo is not acting like "a man" because he does what Sofia wants him to do.

Suggested Essay Topics

1. What insight does Harpo receive about Mr.____'s character? Look at what Mr.____ says to him in this chapter.

2. Why does "a shadow" go across Sofia's face in her argument with Mr.____? What is Harpo's role in this argument?

Letters 19–21

Summary

Harpo wants to know why Sofia will not listen to his orders. Mr.____ tells his son that Sofia needs "a good sound beating." While Celie likes Sofia, she advises Harpo to beat her also. The next time Harpo visits, he is heavily bruised on his face, and walks in on sore legs. Some time after that incident, Celie drops in on Sofia and Harpo's place, only to find them viciously fighting. Their house is devastated from their struggle, and Celie walks back home.

Celie feels guilty for telling Harpo to beat Sofia, and has trouble sleeping for about a month. She understands that her greatest fear is that Sofia will find out. Eventually, Harpo confesses to Sofia that Celie told him to beat her, and Sofia quickly returns the curtains that Celie made for them. When Sofia confronts Celie, Celie admits that she said it because she is jealous of Sofia's strength. Upon hearing this, Sofia calms down and they start to talk candidly. Sofia says that she has had to fight all her life, and that even though she loves Harpo, she will never let any man beat her. She asks Celie how can she stand to live with Mr.____, and Celie responds that she doesn't think about life on earth, since "Heaven last all ways." After Sofia and Celie patch up their differences, they decide to make a quilt out of the curtains that Sofia returned. Celie is now able to sleep at nights.

Analysis

Celie notices how happy Harpo and Sofia seem together. This happiness, however, is due to their contradictory roles in the marriage. Harpo complains about Sofia's refusal to obey, even though he sounds "a little proud of this" to Celie. Mr.____'s advice to Harpo comes from his understanding of a husband-wife relationship and his dislike of Sofia. The fact that Harpo cannot assert himself simply proves to Mr.____ that his son is limited. Celie's advice, however, comes from her jealousy of their relationship. Even though three years pass and he still whistles and sings, Harpo is not satisfied with his role, because he was brought up in a house where the wife was submissive to the husband. When Celie answers the question, she thinks about how "every time I jump when Mr.____ call me, [Sofia] look surprise." She resents Sofia's pity and wants her to feel some of the pain that Celie has always felt. Her advice, however, results in the first humorous event of the entire novel. Harpo's obvious defeat at Sofia's hands should be taken as a lesson. It is futile for Harpo to beat Sofia because they have a happy marriage. If Harpo cannot understand this, he should be able to understand the bruises all over his body, which are some more good reasons not to hit Sofia.

Even though it is clear to everybody what happened to Harpo, he still tries to make lame excuses because he cannot admit he was beaten by a woman. The male and female roles of society, accepted for so long by Mr.____ and Celie, now look out of place when a man like Harpo tries to enforce his will upon Sofia. Sofia proves that even without her sisters to support her, she still has the character to fight for herself. Harpo cannot give up what he has started, because if he cannot make Sofia submit, he will definitely be a failure in the eyes of his father. Sofia, on the other hand, doesn't want to fight Harpo but will not let him treat her as Mr.____ treats Celie. Celie feels responsible for all of this, since her suggestion to Harpo instigated the conflict. Once she sees Sofia's fighting spirit, Celie wishes that she didn't imply that it was proper for Harpo to use violence.

When Sofia finally confides to Celie, she tells a story about her family that serves as a metaphor for the power of unity, which will be a recurring theme in this novel. All the children in Sofia's family were big and strong, and all of them used to fight. But all the girls stick together in the family, which is why Sofia has all the confidence and strength to fight on her own. Celie's upbringing, on the other hand, was isolated. She felt aloof from her brothers and sisters due to her father's rape (which she cannot bring herself to admit to Sofia) and her own feelings of inadequacy brought about by abuse. When Sofia and Celie patch up their differences and begin to make a quilt, they start to form the type of network that Sofia had benefited from since her childhood. The quilt becomes, like the dress Kate made Celie, a symbol of security and togetherness. This togetherness, since both Sofia and Celie contribute to the quilt,

results in a stronger relationship between them. The fact that Celie is able to sleep after she befriends Sofia strengthens the idea that a bond of friendship has been formed. Celie feels more secure at home now because she knows she is not completely alone.

Study Questions

1. Why are Sofia and Harpo arguing at the beginning of this section?

2. Describe Harpo's wounds.

3. What excuse does Harpo give for his wounds?

4. What does Celie do to try to make herself sleep?

5. How much does Sofia pay Celie for use of her curtains?

6. What will happen if Celie continues to advise Harpo?

7. Why does Sofia feel sorry for Celie?

8. How many children does Sofia's father have?

9. What does Celie mean when she tells Sofia that sometimes she has to talk with Old Maker?

10. What does Sofia think Celie should do with Mr.____?

Answers

1. Harpo thinks that Sofia spends too much time with her sister.

2. Harpo has a black eye and a cut lip. He also has a hurt hand and he is walking stiffly.

3. Harpo claims that he was kicked by an angry mule, and then walked into the crib door at home. Then, during the evening, he accidentally closed the window on his hand.

4. Celie tries to stay up as late as possible. Before she goes to bed, she takes a warm bath. Then, she puts a little witch hazel on her pillow and makes sure the room is completely dark. If that doesn't work, she tries drinking a little milk, counting the fence posts, and reading the Bible to fall asleep.

5. Sofia tries to give Celie a dollar for the use of her curtains.

6. Sofia says that if Celie wants a dead son-in-law she should simply keep on advising him like she did before.

7. Celie reminds Sofia of her own mother, who never stood up to her husband.

8. Sofia's father has 12 children—six boys and six girls.

9. Celie means that she talks with God whenever Mr.____ begins to abuse her.

10. Sofia thinks that Celie should kill Mr.____ now and think about heaven later.

Suggested Essay Topics

1. Why wouldn't Harpo want Sofia to visit her sisters? Use examples from the text to support your answer.

2. How would Mr.____ react to Harpo's excuses? Construct a dialogue in which Harpo tries to explain to his father why his face is bruised.

Letters 22–27

New Characters:

Shug Avery: *a nightclub singer, and girlfriend of Mr.____*

Old Mr.____: *Mr.____'s father*

Tobias: *Mr.____'s brother*

Summary

The news goes out all over town that Shug Avery is sick. Nobody wants to take her in, and she has been abandoned by her parents. Furthermore, the town seems to be delighted by Shug's sickness; even the town preacher gives a thinly veiled sermon in which Shug is chastised for her lifestyle. Celie is outraged by this treatment of Shug but does nothing. Mr.____, on the other hand, quickly calls on Harpo to prepare the wagon, and he leaves town.

He returns five days later with Shug Avery, and tells Celie to prepare the guest room.

Mr.___ tries to take care of Shug, but she is weak and unhappy
from her sickness and pushes him away. Celie starts to take care of
Shug on her own, and Shug begins to slowly improve. When Celie
bathes Shug she feels as if she had turned into a man, since she
gets a feeling that she has never had before. Shug starts to eat and
lets Celie comb her hair, which causes her to sing.

While Shug is recovering, Mr.___'s father, who owns the farm
that they work on, visits and complains about Shug's presence.
Mr.___ finds an unexpected ally in Celie during this argument.
Old Mr.___ chastises his son for letting Shug Avery stay and Celie
spits in his water. When Celie and Mr.___ defend Shug against Old
Mr.___ Celie notices that this "is the closest us ever felt" since they
have been married.

When Shug is able to get on her feet, Celie teaches her how to
quilt. They have another visitor at the house, Tobias, Mr.___'s
brother, who presents Shug with a box of chocolates. Everyone is
in a pleasant mood, and as Mr.___, Tobias, Shug, and Celie sit
around talking, Celie says that "for the first time in my life, I feel
just right."

Analysis

The long-awaited appearance of Shug Avery comes after many
instances of foreshadowing, the most dramatic of which is the
announcement that she has fallen ill. Celie finds out about the
town's reaction in the church, which once again becomes a symbol of false protection for women. Even though Celie works hard
to keep the church clean and the priest thanks her by calling her
Sister Celie, Mr.___ uses this opportunity to collect glances from
the neighborhood woman. The priest uses Shug's illness as a cornerstone of his sermon, proving in his eyes that punishment falls
upon the wicked. The irony in this speech is that no one in the
town comes to her defense, even though many of these same
women have been victimized by this type of judgment. The town
is caught up in a display of self-righteousness, and Walker shows
us once again that what takes place in this town's church has little
to do with what takes place in God's kingdom.

Shug Avery's lifestyle was definitely contrary to the standard of behavior that was expected in a rural community. The standards of such a community were exceedingly moral, especially for women. Celie is respected by the church and the preacher because she is a good cook and cleans the church very well. It is never acknowledged that Celie is unhappy with her life. Shug's greatest sin seems to be enjoying herself and not caring what others think. Shug's behavior in many ways (drinking, smoking, and dressing wildly) parallels the behavior of Zora Neale Hurston, a black author who lived during the setting of the novel. Hurston was also criticized for her behavior. Walker, a Hurston scholar, might also be speaking out against the injustice of this moral code because it affected a person who was a gigantic influence upon her life.

When Mr.____ decides to retrieve Shug, the action seems a little hypocritical. Mr.____ can easily shed tears for Shug and say that "nobody fight for" her, even while telling Celie that it "won't do no good" to argue with him about the point. Mr.____'s kind treatment to Shug could be a blow to Celie's pride, but Celie forgets about Mr.____ because Shug, the woman that Celie has been waiting to meet for so long, is finally in their house. The first meeting between Shug and Celie is anticlimactic, with Shug simply looking at Celie and saying "you sure is ugly." Celie had formed a fantasy of Shug in her mind, but it seems that she is just another person in this world that wants nothing to do with her. Celie immediately notices the childlike way she is "evil" towards her and Mr.____. Shug's immaturity is what allows Celie to forget the insult, and to blossom and employ her maternal instincts. Mr.____'s attempts at nursing are pathetic because he thinks of her as a sex object and cannot treat her in a way that requires selflessness and caring. He does care for her, but he is so used to having the upper hand that when he must make another person's concerns first and foremost he simply becomes uncomfortable. Celie, however, is used to having her attention go unnoticed, so Shug's dismissals do not discourage Celie from being affectionate. Shug, in time, is able to respond by appreciating Celie's efforts, either by singing or humming. The relationship between Shug and Celie, which is the cornerstone of the novel, is nurtured very quickly because each one is able to fulfill the other's need. Celie's need is to have somebody to care for, while

Shug needs to have someone who truly cares for her.

Shug's presence, like the presence of a baby, provides the entire home with stability and peace. Since Mr.____ and Celie both love Shug, they now both have something in common. Mr.____ still does not love Celie but is grateful to her for helping Shug. They are able to unite in the conflict with Old Mr.____, who cannot believe that Shug will be anything except disruptive. Old Mr.____ tries to impose his authority by reminding them that he still owns the farm. He also tries to use Celie as a wedge in his son's relationship with Shug. However, both Celie and Mr.____ stand up to Old Mr.____. Even though they do this for Shug's sake rather than for each other, they have nonetheless been able to bridge the gap in their relationship temporarily. This is a testimony to Shug's power.

Shug's greatest accomplishment, however, is to provide Celie with the security that she had started to receive from Sofia. This safety gives Celie confidence because Shug has come with Mr.____'s blessing, and through good fortune she loves Celie as well. Unlike Nettie and Kate, who were quickly removed from Celie's environment, or Sofia, who enjoys an uneasy truce with Mr.____, there is no danger of Shug leaving. So the last scene of this section, in which Celie and Shug start quilting, represents to Celie more than anything else the ideal environment. This makes the last sentence, "For the first time in my life, I feel just right," very significant. She has shown that in the proper environment, she can behave at ease and without compromising her feelings. Shug's presence already has some effect upon Celie. While Tobias visits, Celie notices that he and Old Mr.____ "always talk bout money like they still got a lot," when the real truth is that "[Celie's] and Harpo fields bring in more than anybody." The narrative has become less afraid to tell the truth, and this directly parallels the ease that Celie now feels.

Study Questions

1. What is Shug Avery's nickname?

2. How does the priest characterize Shug in his sermon?

3. Celie says that there is "one good thing" about the fact that Mr.____ doesn't do any work on the farm. What is that thing?

4. How does Shug survive when she is sicker than Celie's mama when she died?

5. How many kids has Shug had with Mr.____?

6. Where are Shug's kids now?

7. Describe Mr.____'s father.

8. What can Mr.____ vouch for about Shug?

9. What does Tobias bring for Shug?

10. Why does Tobias wish his wife, Margaret, was a lot more like Celie?

Answers

1. She is known as the Queen Honeybee.

2. Shug is the nameless "strumpet in short skirts, smoking cigarettes, drinking gin."

3. Since Mr.____ never does work in the field, Celie and Harpo never miss him when he leaves the farm.

4. Celie says that Shug is able to survive because she is "more evil than my mama."

5. Shug Avery has had three children with Mr.____.

6. Shug's children are now staying with her mother.

7. Old Mr.____ is "a little short shrunk up man with a bald head and gold spectacles." He clears his throat "like everything he say need announcement."

8. Mr.____ knows that all of Shug's children have the same father.

9. Tobias brings a box of chocolate for Shug.

10. Tobias wishes that Margaret was "always busy" like Celie so that she could save [him] a bundle of money.

Suggested Essay Topics

1. What symbols of security are present in this section of the novel? How does Celie use such symbols (the bath, food) to comfort Shug?

2. Compare the relationship Mr.____ has with his father to the one that he has with his son. Is there any real difference in these relationships or is it a cycle of abuse from father to son?

Letters 28–31

Summary

One night while Sofia and Celie are making another quilt together, Sofia asks Celie why a man eats. Sofia tells her that Harpo has been eating voraciously for the last few days, even though he isn't hungry. Neither one of them can figure out why he would do this to himself. The next time he visits Celie he begins to go through the pantry and eat whatever food he can get his hands on. Celie doesn't understand this at all, especially since Harpo doesn't seem to be enjoying the food that he is eating.

Harpo grows fat, and one night shows up at Celie's, this time crying and with two black eyes. Celie accuses him of bothering Sofia and wonders why he would do such a thing to a wonderful woman. Harpo admits that Sofia gave him the black eyes but can't understand why she won't listen to him. Harpo wants Sofia to do what he says. Celie quickly tells him that Mr.____ had married her to take care of his children, and that she had no choice in the matter. Celie tells Harpo that Shug, the woman that Mr.____ had wanted to marry, would "tell him his drawers stink in a minute." This revelation makes Harpo cry and vomit, as if he were throwing up "every piece of pie" that he ate.

The next day, Celie visits Sofia, and tells her that Harpo had been eating in order to make himself bigger. He wanted to be as big as his wife, so that he could make her obey him. Sofia sadly nods and admits that she is tired of Harpo. She still loves him but ever since their marriage "all he think about...is how to make [her] mind." She thinks it might be best to visit her sister, Odessa, who is alone now that her husband has been drafted. She tells Celie that she hardly feels anything anymore when she and Harpo have sex, and the worst part is that she thinks he doesn't care. "He git up there and enjoy it just the same. The fact he can do it like that make me want to kill him." Sofia is not sure if she will leave yet, but laughs and says that she definitely needs a vacation.

Eventually, however, Sofia does decide to leave. Her sisters come to pick her up along with her children. Celie decides to give Sofia the quilt they were working on.

Analysis

The situation between Harpo and Sofia has not changed, and the fault lies squarely on Harpo's shoulders. He seems intent on forcing a conflict where none should rightly exist. Sofia is pleased that Harpo enjoys cooking, cleaning, and taking care of the baby. In other words, Harpo enjoys what is considered by society as "women's work." However, this work also compromises his ego, so he cannot receive any satisfaction from this happy marriage. This is ridiculous, of course, but it is the same sort of logic that causes Harpo to force-feed himself. He is torturing himself in order to make himself bigger, so that he can beat up Sofia, even though he doesn't want to hurt her. He has enjoyed his role in the marriage, yet he continually insists that Sofia obey him, even though this insistence will cause the marriage to break up. The root of this problem is Harpo's insecurity. He has already been considered limited by Mr.____, and his inability to control Sofia only adds to this perception. He was brought up in a house where he learned that "the wife spose to mind," but he doesn't understand that Celie doesn't love Mr.____. He connects Sofia's refusal to obey with a lack of love. Celie points out that the rightful analogy should be Mr.____'s relationship with Shug Avery, since this relationship is based upon love, and Shug certainly does not obey Mr.____'s every wish.

The reader notices the change in Celie's character that has come about due to her relationships with Sofia and Shug. Earlier, Celie had tried to drive a wedge between Sofia and Harpo. Now, she is open with Harpo in an attempt to reconcile them. She also is able to be frank about her own feelings without fear, which is a sharp contrast to the timid advice she offers Harpo earlier. The text in this language is also stronger, which is consistent with Celie's

new confidence. She says with a little venom in her voice that Harpo looks like a "retard" and actually shakes him in order to make him understand her words. She has never been so aggressive before. Now she knows that she has something important to say, especially to a fool like Harpo.

When Sofia does leave, she still has her network of support to maintain her strength. Her sisters come to get her, indicating that she will not suffer as much from the separation. Celie wishes for Nettie when she hears that Sofia will leave with her sisters, showing that while she has benefited from her new friends, there is still a gap in her heart for her sister. Celie is strong enough to provide Sofia with a quilt, however, and for the first time helps another woman with a symbol of protection. This proves that Celie has grown stronger during the novel, and the support that she has received has allowed her to become a protector as well. The theme of growth had been implied in previous sections but is now developed through Celie and Sofia. This theme has been developed with the giving and receiving gifts, which imply protection. At the beginning of her marriage, Celie could only take things from others (Kate and Nettie) because she was too weak to provide others with anything. Sofia, on the other hand, could not accept a gift from Celie. She had also led a tough life, which caused her to look to her sisters for help but no one else. As Sofia leaves, we see that Celie can now provide someone with protection (a quilt), while Sofia now trusts others. Their relationship has allowed them both to be less afraid of others and to develop personally.

Study Questions

1. What reasons does Celie give for eating?

2. What is clabber?

3. List what Harpo eats when he visits Celie.

4. What is meant when Harpo is asked "When is it due?"

5. Where does Harpo end up sleeping after his fight with Sofia?

6. After Harpo and Sofia fight, Harpo appears at Celie's house with two black eyes. What bruises does Sofia have?

7. When Mr.____ and Celie have sex, how long does it take for both of them to fall asleep?

8. What does Sofia take when she leaves?

9. Describe Sofia's sisters.

10. What does Harpo pretend to do while Sofia packs up her things?

Answers

1. Celie says that some people eat because "food taste good," while others "love to feel they mouth work." Sometimes, it also "might be a case of being undernourish."

2. Clabber is the thick, sour milk that collects on a butter churn.

3. Harpo eats a piece of fried chicken, a slice of blueberry pie, a glass of clabber, and a slice of cornbread.

4. Harpo has become so fat that he begins to look like he is pregnant.

5. Harpo sleeps in a bed next to Shug's room.

6. Sofia has only a scratch on her wrist.

7. Both Celie and Mr.____ are asleep in ten minutes.

8. Sofia takes the children and their clothes, as well as her own clothes. In addition she takes a mattress, a looking glass, and a rocking chair.

9. To Celie, Sofia's sisters "look like amazons."

10. Harpo is pretending to make a fish net while he is waiting for Sofia to leave.

Suggested Essay Topics

1. What are some of the chores that Harpo does? What insight does the reader receive into Harpo's character with respect to these chores?

2. What role does food play in this section? What is it a symbol for? Use examples from the text to support your conclusion.

Letters 32–36

New Characters:

Swain: *Harpo's friend*

Henry "Buster" Broadnax: *Sofia's new companion*

Squeak (Mary Agnes): *Harpo's new girlfriend*

Summary

Six months after Sofia leaves, Harpo has become a different man. He takes his old house, and builds a jukejoint (bar and night-club) along with his partner, Swain. No one comes to the new place, so Harpo begs Shug to perform at his bar. Shug, who by now has almost fully recovered, agrees to perform, and the club fills up in anticipation of her arrival.

Celie is excited that she will finally get an opportunity to hear Shug perform. Mr.____ does not want Celie to be there, but Shug insists upon it. Celie and Mr.____ sit down at the same table, and Shug begins to sing a song that is meant for Mr.____. Celie starts to cry without understanding why, and then she realizes that Shug loves Mr.____ more than Celie. Then she hears Shug yelling Celie's name. Shug announces to the crowd that she has written a new song, called "Miss Celie's Song." It is the same tune that Shug was humming when Celie fixed her hair. Celie hums along with the tune, saying that it is the "first time somebody made something and named it after me."

Now that Shug is well, she tells Celie that she will probably leave soon, but then she sees that Celie is scared. Celie tells Shug that Mr.____ will probably start beating her again. Shug vows that she will stay until she knows Albert won't even think about beating Celie. Shug also asks Celie if it matters to her that she sleeps with her husband. Celie says she doesn't mind because she never en- joys sex with Mr.____ anyway. Upon hearing this, Shug is surprised. She asks Celie if she has ever seen herself naked. Even though Celie is embarrassed, Shug asks Celie to examine herself in the looking glass. She tells Celie that women have a "button" "...that gits real hot when you do you know what with somebody." Celie examines herself and gingerly touches her "button," which gives her a feeling that she has never felt before. After she discovers this, however, she becomes sad when she can hear Shug and Mr.___ making love in the next room.

One night in the club, Sofia walks in with her new friend, a big man named Buster. Sofia is overjoyed to see everybody, especially Celie, but then Harpo, who has become fat once again, wants to know why Sofia is there. Sofia says she just wanted to hear Shug sing. Harpo asks Sofia to dance, which enrages his new girlfriend, Squeak. Squeak tries to attack Sofia, and loses two teeth. Squeak orders Harpo to kick out Sofia, but Harpo just stands between them, unable to decide. Finally, Harpo tends to Squeak's wounds while Sofia and Buster "get out the door and don't look back."

Analysis

Sofia's departure causes Harpo to revert to old stereotypes of masculine behavior. He replaces his wife with a male friend and proceeds to build a nightclub, the name of which indicates his ego and self-importance. The fact that he creates the nightclub out of his old house is proof that he has rejected his previous life as husband. Harpo also shows that he has a flair for business, as he and Swain tell Celie the advantages of having the club in a relatively secluded place. Harpo recognizes that it is possible to make money within the black community. The elaborate reworking of his club, however, does not mean that the club is a success. The club's initial failure shows that Harpo is still the same sort of man without Sofia, a man whose self-worth is much greater than his actual worth. It is Shug's performances that make the club a success. Even though Harpo will never admit it, he needs a strong woman to compensate for his own weakness. His chauvinism will continue to stand in the way of his success.

This chauvinism is also evident in his choice of a new girlfriend. Squeak reminds Celie of herself, mostly because "she do everything Harpo say." She approaches Harpo's ideal of a woman more closely than Sofia ever did, which makes the fight all the more surprising. Even though Sofia never listened to Harpo, he still cannot get over her. Yet he continues to be with a girl that he can dominate, just

because his need to stroke his ego is greater than the love that he shared with Sofia. The irony is that getting respect from Squeak does not mean anything to the other people in his life. Harpo is not respected because he was big enough a fool to let Sofia go, and his dominance of Squeak was almost predicted by Celie in the previous section. The cycle started by men in this novel is now complete; just as Mr.____ loves Shug and oppresses Celie, Harpo loved Sofia but now oppresses Squeak. Celie (and the reader) cannot understand why Harpo would continue to make himself unhappy just so that he can think of himself as a dominant male. If Harpo really just wanted a woman who would do whatever he said, love notwithstanding, he doesn't prove it by chasing after Sofia, who has found a man that will give her the freedom that she wants.

This conflict is paralleled by Shug's performances on stage, which become the center of a conflict between Celie and Mr.____. Mr.____ has already tried to enforce his wishes upon Celie by keeping her from the club; Shug's insistence, however, is more powerful to Mr.____ than Nettie or Kate's influence, so he gives in. Shug responds to his complaints about how his wife should behave by saying "Good thing I ain't your damn wife." This statement not only quiets him, but also reminds him who has the upper hand in their relationship. There is no legal bond to which Shug feels any obligation. This put-down also implies that whoever is his "damn wife" is suffering under his thumb. Shug presents support for Celie at a time when her previous would-be defenders were easily dismissed by Mr.____.

When Celie and Mr.____ watch Shug at the club, however, we see where Shug's allegiance is. Celie describes Mr.____ as a "little man, all puff[ed] up," indicating that this is an insecure man who loves the attention of others because it makes him feel bigger. He is proud of himself because he is Shug's lover. His domination of those weaker than he reveals his insecurity. At the club, Celie feels that it is unfair that all of these people talk to Mr.____ not knowing what sort of person he actually is. To add insult to injury, Shug dedicates a song to Albert, which causes Celie to cry. She is surprised by her crying but then understands that she feels Shug's apparent choice of Mr.____ is a rejection of her. Celie hates to lose Shug to her husband because Celie has already been deprived of so much by him. Even though she understands that Albert is Shug's lover and "that the way it spose to be," this rejection is unexpected, because she has finally allowed herself to be open towards somebody else. However, Shug's song to Celie afterwards is a reward for Celie's loyalty and trust, and an example of Shug's loyalty to her own friend.

This loyalty keeps Shug near Celie when she finds out that Celie is abused by Mr.____. Upon hearing this for the first time, Shug is shocked. This causes her to focus her loyalty upon Celie both as a friend and as a woman. Shug hates the thought of a crime committed against a woman, especially against one that she cares about. She vows to protect her, and form the same sort of network that Sofia always had. In addition to this, Shug is responsible for Celie's self-awareness of her body. The fact that Celie can derive pleasure by simply manipulating a "button" is a symbol of Mr.____'s ignorance and lack of respect for his wife. Celie never enjoyed sex, and has always been used by men rather than a participant in mutual pleasure. Celie's simile of Mr.____'s act (going to the toilet) is very appropriate in this case; the irony is that deriving pleasure from sex would have been easy if Celie had a caring partner. Now that she knows that it is very simple to enjoy sex, she becomes upset when Shug and Albert have sex together. Mr.____ could have provided Celie with pleasure but chose not to, which naturally bothers her.

Study Questions

1. What is the name of Harpo's new club?
2. Why is Harpo puzzled by Shug?
3. How does Shug describe the first time she made love with Mr.____?
4. What does having sex with Mr.____ feel like to Celie?
5. What was the best thing about having children for Celie?
6. How does Shug act like a man?
7. What does Harpo consider a scandal?
8. What is Buster's "job," with regards to Sofia?

9. How did Squeak get her nickname?

10. What does "teenouncy" mean?

Answers

1. Harpo's new club is called "Harpo's."

2. Harpo is confused by Shug's willingness to say whatever she feels. Harpo's ideal woman would behave like Celie, and do whatever he wants her to do. Harpo still cannot handle an independent woman.

3. Shug says that the first time was an accident. Feeling carried them away.

4. Celie says it feels like Mr.____ is going to the toilet on her.

5. Celie loved to nurse her children because she used to feel a shiver.

6. Shug talks like a man; instead of talking about hair or health, she compliments another woman on her good looks. Celie becomes slightly aroused when she sees Shug walking around in the club.

7. Harpo thinks that it is "a scandless" that "a woman with five children (Sofia) [is] hanging out in a jukejoint at night."

8. Buster's job is "to love (Sofia) and take her where she want to go."

9. Harpo gave Squeak that nickname, presumably because of her voice.

10. "Teenouncy" is a cross between tiny and bouncy, which accurately describes Squeak's voice.

Suggested Essay Topics

1. What is the significance of Harpo's weight? Compare this to the time he tries to gain weight in order to fight Sofia.

2. How does Shug's knowledge that Mr.____ had beat Celie change their relationship? Can you predict the changes that will take place in the future?

Letters 37–41

New Characters:

Odessa: *Sofia's sister*

Miss Millie: *the mayor's wife*

The Mayor: *town official*

Summary

Squeak asks Celie why Harpo has been so morose lately, and Celie tells her about the scandal that has shocked the entire family. Sofia has been arrested for attacking the mayor. One day she went to town with Buster and the children when the mayor's wife stopped them. The mayor's wife, Miss Millie, coos over Sofia's children. She thinks that they are so cute, she asks Sofia if she wants to be her maid. When Sofia refuses, the mayor slaps her for not being respectful. Mr.____ simply says "you know what happen if somebody slap Sofia" and Celie doesn't feel the need to say anything else. Squeak can't believe it, so Celie tries to tell her how Sofia is beaten within an inch of her life, and how Buster is powerless to help Sofia because the police have drawn their guns on him.

Sofia is sentenced to 12 years in prison, and spends her time working in the prison laundry. When everybody goes to visit her, she says that she survives by pretending that she is Celie, and simply doing just what they say. She tries to joke about this but Celie notices that "she look wild" when she admits this. Celie, Shug, Mr.____, Squeak, Buster, and Sofia's sisters get together after supper and agree that Sofia will not be able to survive jail. They try to come up with a plan of escape.

After a few plans are dismissed, Squeak admits that the warden is actually her uncle. After hearing this, it is decided that Squeak will go to her uncle and complain that Sofia is not being treated harshly enough. Squeak is washed and dressed up in some of Shug's clothes in order to help her "convince" the warden that Sofia would suffer even more as the mayor's maid.

Squeak returns from the warden's office in a ripped dress. Harpo is incensed to learn that the warden took liberties with her and threatens to set fire to the place. Squeak quiets Harpo, and tells the rest of the group that she was raped by her own uncle. She also tells Harpo her real name: Mary Agnes.

Analysis

This section of the novel focuses upon Sofia's downfall. It seemed that Sofia was the one character who was sure of herself and what she was doing. This was directly connected with the support she received from her sisters, her children, and her new boyfriend. However, when Sofia gets caught in this situation, she becomes involved in a society in which both she and her family find that they have less influence. Her frank talk is interpreted as insubordination and her ability to defend herself is called assault, not simply because she is a black woman striking a white person but also since that person is the mayor, and therefore a man in an ultimate position of power. As a result, she is mercilessly beaten at the hands of the police. Even Mr.____ and Harpo, who have been using their positions of strength to abuse women, are disgusted.

This irony, however, is lost in the desire to free Sofia. Sofia, meanwhile, without her friends close by, immediately adopts a Celie-like persona, and provides insight to Celie's character. We learn that Sofia does everything that she is told merely to survive. She is completely isolated and can now count on no one for support, yet she still thinks that she can live through it and eventually be reunited with the children. This parallels Celie's belief that even when she had no one to support her, she must endure life with Mr.____ in order to enter Heaven and be eternally happy. Since most of Sofia's friends and family reject this idea and feel she must escape now, we can conclude that the same sort of escape will eventually be necessary for Celie. However, when a plan for escape is called for, Celie can only daydream about God blowing a big breath of fire to free Sofia, indicating that she still relies on a miracle to make everyone righteous and everything normal.

However, Sofia's network of support is still active outside of the jail, and they work hard to find an area within the system that they are able to manipulate. When Squeak confesses that she is the niece of one of the wardens, the rest in the group propel her to act on Sofia's behalf, something that she might not be willing to do

on her own. The strength of the group lies in its love of Sofia, and even though Squeak is no friend to Sofia, those that love both Sofia and Squeak are able to bridge the gap and support her. Men participate in this group for the first time, proving that they are capable of support as well. Sofia had talked about this long ago with Celie; when her sisters fought her brothers, one or two brothers would join Sofia and her sisters, and then they were unstoppable. The strength of this force is also implied by the participation of Mr.____ and Buster.

This is the first section in which Walker illustrates the disparity of black and white societies. Mr.____ tries to help Sofia by going to see the sheriff, whom he knows. However, Mr.____ does not appeal to the sheriff by telling him of the injustice; he simply agrees with the sheriff that Sofia is crazy in hope of winning some sympathy. The relationship between Mr.____ and the sheriff is civil only because Mr.____ "know he colored," that is, he recognizes his inferior position in society. Another example of this inequity occurs when Squeak confesses that her father is white, and the brother of the warden. Buster finds the entire plan distasteful, and calls it "Uncle Tomming," but just as Mr.____ must maintain a subservient role when talking to the sheriff, Sofia's friends can only aid her within the context of an unfair society. There isn't much else anybody can do.

Walker also introduced the fact that white males often had children with black women without accepting the responsibility of the children. This is represented when the warden denies the fact that he is Squeak's uncle. Furthermore, he rapes her, while proclaiming that if he were her uncle, it would be a sin to do so. Symbolically, this is not the first time that Squeak has been taken advantage of by whites; what was done to her through societal laws is now done to her physically.

The cruelty of society upon the weak, and upon the blacks, is exhibited by Squeak's rape at the hands of the warden. However, Squeak, to the surprise of the others, becomes stronger after this abuse. This is shown by her adoption of her given name, Mary Agnes. Celie had insisted to Squeak that she make Harpo call her by her real name, and "then maybe he see you when he trouble," but Squeak did not understand what Celie meant. This attack by the warden causes Squeak to drop her nickname, which implied that she was the girl that did whatever her man wanted. Squeak was the woman that was raped, but now with her new identity, not only will she no longer be the girl that was an easy target of abuse and manipulation, but she will also stand up for herself against any future indignities.

Study Questions

1. How does Harpo mope?

2. What does Miss Millie always do, according to her husband?

3. What does Buster do while Sofia is getting beaten?

4. When the sheriff says that Sofia is crazy, how does Mr.____ reply?

5. How badly is Sofia injured from her beating by the police?

6. Who takes care of Sofia's children while Sofia is in jail?

7. How often is Sofia visited by her friends?

8. What does Squeak remember about her uncle?

9. What is the warden's justification for what he does to Squeak?

10. What does Mary Agnes mean when she asks Harpo if he loves her or her color?

Answers

1. Harpo is quiet and spends most of his time walking up and down the aisle in his club. He also totally ignores Squeak despite her best efforts to get him to say something.

2. The mayor says that Miss Millie is "always going on over colored" children.

3. Sofia keeps Buster from joining in the fight and tells him to look after the children. She knows that with six armed policemen around them, Buster would have been shot if he had tried to make any aggressive move.

4. Mr.____ tells the sheriff that he had tried to tell his son for 12 years that Sofia was crazy. He doesn't really believe this

now, but he is trying to keep on friendly terms with the sheriff in case something can be done for Sofia.

5. Sofia's skull and ribs are cracked, and one eye has been blinded. Her nose has also been torn, and her entire body is swollen.

6. Odessa and Squeak take care of Sofia's children.

7. Sofia gets visitors two times a month for half an hour.

8. A few years ago, her uncle gave Squeak and her siblings each a quarter.

9. The warden says that if he is really Squeak's uncle, what he is doing would be a sin, but "everybody guilty...of a little fornication."

10. Squeak wants Harpo to know that she is a woman with a strong character, and that if he only loves her superficially, because of her appearance, then he can leave right now. Mary Agnes insists that Harpo respect the person on the inside.

Suggested Essay Topics

1. How does Walker use Sofia's beating to illustrate the danger of being a woman in a male-dominated society?

2. Use examples from the text, including Squeak's dialogue, to show her transformation in character.

3. Have you ever had a personal experience when a tragedy proved to be beneficial in the long run?

Letters 42–44

New Characters:

Eleanor Jane: *the young daughter of Miss Millie*

Billy: *the young son of Miss Millie*

Jack: *Odessa's husband*

Summary

Six months have passed since they tried to use Squeak to get Sofia out of jail. Mary Agnes surprises everybody by starting to sing some songs that she wrote. She soon becomes very popular, and everyone discovers that she has a good singing voice. Harpo can't understand why she sings now when she had been so quiet the year before, but he doesn't object.

Meanwhile, Sofia has been released from prison under the condition that she work for the mayor and Miss Millie as their maid. Three years after she starts working for them, she is sitting in Miss Millie's yard with Celie. She is talking about how angry she feels while she is watching the mayor's children play ball. She asks Celie why "we ain't already kill off" all the white people, and Celie replies that there are simply "too many." While Sofia and Celie are talking, Billy, the mayor's six-year-old son, orders Sofia to get a ball for him. When Sofia ignores him, he runs over to kick Sofia's leg. He misses, and cuts his foot on a rusty nail. Miss Millie runs out to find out what happened, even though she is scared of Sofia. Eleanor Jane, the younger daughter, quickly defends Sofia. Celie notices that the little girl clearly loves Sofia, even though it doesn't matter to Sofia at all.

Another time, Sofia tells Celie about a different incident with Miss Millie. The mayor presented Miss Millie with a new car but Millie does not know how to drive, so she asks Sofia to teach her. After a while, Millie is a good driver and is so grateful to Sofia that she decides to take her to see her children, since it has been five years and Sofia still hasn't seen her children. Sofia readily agrees, but Millie insists that she sit in the back seat before she drives her to Odessa and Jack's house, because Millie is afraid of how she will look if she lets a black woman sit alongside her. Once they arrive there, however, Millie is trapped because she doesn't know how to drive in reverse. Sofia tries to teach her how to back up. After a long time, the engine gives out. Millie refuses to be driven home by Jack alone, so Sofia is forced to accompany them. Sofia's day with her family turns out to be 15 minutes long. Sofia chuckles sadly after remembering that incident and tells Celie that "White folks is a miracle of affliction."

Analysis

We see a reversal of sorts in the roles of Mary Agnes and Sofia. Mary Agnes surprises everyone when she starts to sing. The only other woman who sings in this novel is Shug Avery, and she is the strongest character in this novel. Shug has been able to take her pain and her emotions and turn them into powerful statements of song. Mary Agnes is now able to do the same, a symbol of her newly found independence. Her song is also a cry out for self-identity.

The line "they calls me yellow like yellow be my name" means that Mary Agnes feels that too many people identify her by her light skin. Since there is more to her than her light skin, she wonders "why ain't black the same." It is ironic that even though blacks think of her as yellow, she is still considered black by the white South. In the first half of the twentieth century, any child of a union between a black person and white person was still considered black, regardless of skin color. Squeak wishes to clarify her own identity in light of perceptions of both white and black society. She is a light-skinned black woman, yet people have focused upon the fact that her skin is light. She would rather be known as black if her color is used as her name. This song is evidence that she has a stronger sense of self. Even bull-headed Harpo is impressed by her new strength.

This sense of self is taken away from Sofia when she begins work as the mayor's maid. She is forced into a role that she doesn't want, a stereotypically weak role that keeps her isolated from her family and friends. This clearly has an effect on her psyche. Celie notices on her rare visits that Sofia no longer laughs. The environment in which she works is so alienating that the support she occasionally receives from the little girl is unnoticed. Even though she teaches Miss Millie how to drive, her work is unappreciated. In Miss Millie's society, blacks are simply not considered equals. Miss Millie uses up Sofia's life to learn how to drive and repays her cheaply with 15 minutes of time with her family. Miss Millie, however, only remembers that she was willing to drive Sofia to her family, and considers this a monumental act of kindness. Millie does not understand the role that Sofia's family plays in her life, and that Sofia's son looks upon his mother as a captive of the mayor's family. Millie feels Sofia is ungrateful. She has given her a job instead of jail, not realizing that there is not much difference between the two.

When Sofia is finally allowed time with her family, she is pulled back because Miss Millie can't start the car without her. We see that her position in her own family has been usurped by her position as maid. All the help she gave to her children and sisters is now taken by the ungrateful Miss Millie. The reader knows that the help is unappreciated because Millie won't accept help from Jack or Odessa, on the grounds that she doesn't know them. The reader knows by now that help from Sofia's sisters is as good as help from Sofia herself, but Millie is too limited by prejudice to see this. It is this same prejudice that forces her to ask Sofia to sit in the back seat.

Sofia has gone from being a strong character to being one thwarted by social status; Millie is afraid that Sofia would be perceived as an equal. In return for these suspicions, Sofia has to provide Millie with all of her care and support, even though it goes unreturned. Without the love that she can count on from her family, Sofia becomes identified only by her color, which is the same fate that Mary Agnes now fights against.

Study Questions

1. Who writes the songs that Mary Agnes sings?

2. Is Mary Agnes still mad that Sofia knocked out her teeth?

3. Why do Sofia's children love Mary Agnes?

4. Why does Celie consider it impossible to "kill off" the whites?

5. Why does Miss Millie ask the mayor for a car?

6. How does the mayor get revenge for Millie's insistence?

7. What does Miss Millie mean when she tells Sofia that "this is the South"?

8. How do all of Sofia's children react when she shows up?

9. What does Miss Millie intend to do?

10. What actually happens that day with Sofia and Millie?

Answers

1. At first, Mary Agnes sings Shug's songs, then she starts writing her own songs.

2. Mary Agnes is still mad, but she understands Sofia's situation.

3. Sofia's children love Mary Agnes because she lets them do what they want, which is a big difference from the way Odessa or any other of Sofia's sisters treat them.

4. Celie thinks that there are just "too many to kill off."

5. Miss Millie feels that "if colored could have cars than one for her was past due."

6. The mayor buys Millie a car but doesn't teach her how to drive. Every night he rubs it in by asking his wife how she is "enjoying" her car, knowing she doesn't have any friends to teach her.

7. Millie objects to Sofia sitting in the front seat with her, when in the South, one usually doesn't see "a white person and a colored sitting side by side in a car, when one of them wasn't showing the other one how to drive it or clean it." Millie doesn't want Sofia in a position of being an equal, now that she isn't teaching her.

8. No one knew Sofia was coming, and only the two eldest children remember her and come up to hug her. Then all the little children start to hug her as well.

9. Miss Millie was going to leave Sofia at Odessa's house and then return at five to pick her up.

10. Jack and Sofia have to drive Millie back to the mayor's house in Jack's pickup, and then Jack and Sofia drive into town to find a mechanic. Finally, Sofia drives Miss Millie's car back to her house at five o'clock.

Suggested Essay Topics

1. What does Miss Millie's car symbolize in this novel?

2. Why is Miss Millie always "scared" to come in contact with Sofia?

Letters 45–48

New Character:

Grady: *Shug's new husband*

Summary

Shug has been on the road and making money, and is now very successful. She writes to Mr.____ and Celie that she is coming home for Christmas and has a big surprise for them. Mr.____ and Celie are shocked to discover that the surprise is Grady, Shug's new husband. Celie knows "the minute she say [that they are married] that I don't like Grady." Nevertheless, they make him feel welcome. Mr.____ spends most of the vacation drinking with him.

Celie spends a lot of time talking with Shug, who now owns a house in Memphis and 100 pretty dresses. Shug asks her if she has had a better life with Mr.____ ever since Shug convinced him not to hit his wife anymore. Celie says that he tries "to play with the button but...don't git nowhere." Celie guesses that she is still a virgin.

When the talk turns to sex, Celie reminisces to Shug about the time she was raped by her father. She had hidden the pain and shame of it for so long that she begins to weep when she tells Shug about it. She goes on to cry out against Mr.____, who always "clam on top of me" without once thinking about how she feels. When she finishes, she morosely says that "nobody ever love me." Shug replies "I love you, Miss Celie," and kisses her. Celie, at first surprised, then kisses Shug back, and they continue to kiss each other and touch each other until they fall asleep in each other's arms.

When everyone gets together for a party, Shug once again compliments Mary Agnes on her beautiful voice, and begins to advise her on a singing career. Harpo starts to object, but Shug quickly dismisses him. Shug also notices that Grady keeps "making goo-goo eyes at Squeak," but doesn't draw attention to it. Celie tries to like Grady but finds that there is "one thing I sure nuff can't stand, the way he call Shug Mama."

Analysis

Shug's marriage brings a moment of crisis to the novel, and to the lives of Celie and Mr.____. For Mr.____, her marriage is a rejection of him and his life, since he has devoted himself to Shug. It also proves that Shug is able to resist his control. However, another question is brought up by Shug's marriage. How will the marriage affect her character? After the debilitating effect Mr.____ and Harpo have upon the women they marry, the reader becomes suspicious of Grady and his effect upon Shug. Shug never seemed to be the type of person to marry, since we connect marriage with ideas such as sacrifice and compromise.

Perhaps this change in character is brought about by Shug's new success as a singer. Now that she has money, she might have to surround herself with the trappings of success, such as the new car and the new husband. There is a lot of evidence to suggest that Shug's new marriage is a selling out, a marriage that is made so that she might be perceived as a normal woman in society. Grady is certainly not a dominating character; Shug seems to have control over the relationship. Grady calls Shug "Mama" and is dependent on her for money and things as if she were his mother. Celie's first reaction to all of this is that she has been betrayed; Shug seems to have abandoned her previous life in favor of these new possessions.

This question is ultimately resolved, however, by the consummation of love between Celie and Shug. It is Shug's love that finally allows Celie to confront her rape and the injustices of her life. She can now expect more from life because she has someone who can share in her life. Shug and Celie fulfill each other in a way that Mr.____ could never fulfill Celie. Celie is kissed tenderly by Shug, as the lover that Mr.____ never could be, and she can confide in Shug, like the sister that Mr.____ took away. Shug even sucks on Celie's nipple like "one of [her] little lost babies," filling the emptiness that came when Celie's father stole her children.

After Shug behaves this way towards Celie, it is clear that the marriage to Grady is merely camouflage, almost an act of spite towards Mr.____. Shug hasn't felt the same way about Mr.____ since she heard about his abuse of Celie, and the one clear result of her marriage to Grady is that it removes Mr.____ from her life. Grady

and Shug's relationship seems to be very loose, as Shug isn't even bothered by her husband's apparent interest in Squeak. What this marriage does is give Shug freedom to pursue more personal relationships between women without disapproval from society. Having apparently closed her male relationships off by marrying Grady, a man who allows her to do as she wishes, she is now free to deepen her bond with Celie, a person she truly loves.

Music also plays a role in this chapter, as Shug tries to convince Mary Agnes to sing more often in public. She encourages Squeak to sing so-called "devil's music," meaning the blues, because this type of music is very erotic and sensual. In advocating this type of music, she disparages the singing in church, which is made by "funny voices." The images that Shug raises of devils will become more important once her religious beliefs are revealed. For now, she sounds as if she is against religion and God and in favor of hedonism.

Study Questions

1. What does Mr.____ think the surprise will be?
2. What doesn't Celie like about Grady at their first meeting?
3. How did Shug and Grady meet?
4. What would Shug do if she were Celie's husband?
5. Why does Shug ask Celie if they could sleep together?
6. What are the "freakish things" that Shug thought was only done by "white folks"?
7. What does sleeping with Shug feel like to Celie?
8. How does Grady spend Shug's money, according to Celie?
9. Where is Grady from?
10. What does Shug mean when she tells Harpo that his nightclub singer "can't get her ass out the church"?

Answers

1. Mr.____ thinks that Shug bought him a new car.
2. Celie doesn't like Grady's shape, teeth, clothes, or his smell.

3. Grady was the mechanic who fixed Shug's new car.

4. Shug would work hard for Celie and "cover [her] up with kisses stead of licks" if she were her husband.

5. Mr.____ and Grady go out for a night on the town, and Shug doesn't like to sleep alone.

6. Celie's father had raped her while she was cutting his hair, and soon he wants her to cut his hair every time he has sex with her. Shug believed that only "white folks" could be so perverted.

7. Celie tries to compare sleeping with Shug to sleeping with Nettie and her mother, but it feels too different. She decides that it feels "like heaven...not like sleeping with Mr.____ at all."

8. Celie thinks that Grady spends Shug's money as if he made it himself.

9. Grady is from Memphis, Tennessee.

10. The singer's voice sounds like a woman in a choir, but Shug thinks that good music is "devil's music." Shug likes Squeak's singing because when people hear her singing, "folks git to thinking bout a good screw."

Suggested Essay Topics

1. How does Shug's idea of music compare with her character? Look for examples of music and songs as symbols in this novel.

2. How has Harpo diminished in his role as husband and as a male in this society? Compare his dialogue in this section to earlier sections.

Letters 49–51

Summary

Shug asks Celie many questions about Nettie, because Nettie
was the only girl Celie ever loved. Celie tells her that she has been
waiting every day for all of these years for a letter from Nettie, but
she never wrote. After this conversation, Shug starts hanging out
with Mr.____ again, which shocks and pains Grady and Celie.

It soon becomes clear why Shug is doing this, however. After a
week Shug gives Celie a letter from Nettie, which Mr.____ took out
of his mailbox and hid in his coat pocket. Obviously, Mr.____ has
been hiding these letters from Celie all of this time. Hearing about
this causes Celie to temporarily lose her mind. She fantasizes about
murdering him, and even approaches him from behind with a razor when she is stopped by Shug. Shug tries to calm down Celie by
telling her about the time when she was young and courted by
Albert. Shug confesses that she was an evil girl who tortured Annie
Julia, Mr.____'s last wife, and Celie, even though she didn't want to
marry him herself. Shug cannot believe that Albert, the man she
knew, could turn into this monster, and she also cannot believe
that she loved him.

Celie and Shug realize that there might be more letters hidden
in Mr.____'s trunk, and they search the trunk the next time Grady
and Mr.____ go out on the town. They find dozens of letters from
Nettie hidden in the bottom of the trunk. They steam open the letters and place the empty envelopes back into Mr.____'s trunk. Shug
begins to arrange the letters and Celie begins to read them.

Analysis

The action of the novel takes an unexpected turn with the surprise return of Nettie. The effect on Celie is profound, affecting her
even when years of cruelty and abuse could never provoke a response.

Celie first receives a mild shock when she thinks that Shug has
gone back to Mr.____. She deals with this betrayal with the same
ineffective method that she uses for all her crises: praying. This use

of prayer has always been ineffective because she has never truly believed in it. Once she receives Nettie's letter and hears how Mr.____ has kept her sister from her all these years, she finally reacts as she wanted to when she was first abused. Her repressed anger comes forth, and only the interference of Shug keeps Celie from doing something drastic. The visions of murder that Celie sees are not only a result of the abuse she has received from him but from the men in her life since she was born.

Shug, for her part, begins a long narrative about her youth, when she knew Mr.____ as Albert. We learn that Albert was repressed as a young man, and that their relationship suffered interference from Albert's family. Albert's parents treated him in the same manner as he treated his own son when he wanted to marry Sofia. Shug uses this story so that we may understand Albert's cruelty, even though we don't find him any more sympathetic as a character. Shug repeats that Albert was weak, and not the ogre that he is now. His cruelty, therefore, is a manifestation of his weakness. He began to lash out against people he knew wouldn't fight back, such as Annie Julia, his first wife. His control over others was made easier by Shug's own cruelty, a cruelty that came from her independence rather than her weakness. Shug was blinded by love for Albert, and used this love as a weapon against Annie Julia. The fact that she doesn't love Albert now causes her to be racked with guilt for how mean and wild she used to be. In light of what had happened, it seems to her as if she was cruel to the people to whom she should have been kindest. Shug's support of Celie in her angriest hour shows the transition she has made, in which Celie played a large part.

Study Questions

1. What do stamps look like, according to Celie?
2. What does Nettie's letter look like?
3. How does Shug cover for Celie's theft of Mr.____'s razor?
4. What is Shug's real name, and why is she called Shug?
5. Describe Shug's relationship with her parents.
6. What did Shug's sister do for a living?

7. List the things Albert used to do when he went out with Shug.

8. How does Shug describe Annie Julia?

9. Why did Shug want Albert to choose her?

10. What does Shug mean when she says "what was good tween us must have been nothing but bodies?"

Answers

1. Celie thinks that all stamps look the same, with "white men with long hair" on them.

2. Nettie's letter, according to Celie, has "little fat queen of England stamps on it, plus stamps that got peanuts, coconuts, rubber trees and say Africa" on it.

3. Shug takes the razor from Celie's hand and thanks her for getting something to take care of her hangnail. Then she puts the razor back in the shaving box.

4. Shug's real name is Lillie, but everyone called her Shug because she was "just so sweet."

5. Her mother did not like physical contact with her children, and would always push Shug away if she tried to kiss her. Although her father liked to hold her, Shug's mother kept that from happening. Shug admits that she was happy to find Albert so that she could have somebody to hold.

6. Shug's sister worked in a roadhouse as a cook.

7. There are two things that Shug remembers about Albert when he was young. He used to dance all the time, sometimes for an hour. He always used to make Shug laugh.

8. Annie Julia was a beautiful girl, with "big black eyes look like moons." Shug also says that she was "black as anything, and skin just as smooth."

9. Shug felt the need for Albert to choose her because she felt that "nature had already done it."

10. Shug means that it felt so nice physically that she must not have paid attention to his character. She can hardly believe that she went out with and loved such a cruel man.

Suggested Essay Topics

1. Comment on the behavior of Shug's and Albert's parents. How does it compare with the behavior of Mr.____ as a father and Celie's parents? What sort of cycle is being perpetuated?

2. What is found in Mr.____'s trunk? What is symbolized by the trunk and the objects found inside?

Letters 52–60

New Character:

Adam: *Celie's lost son, now the adopted son of Samuel and Corrine*

Summary

Celie reads Nettie's adventures since leaving the farm of Mr.____. The next letters are read from Nettie's point of view.

Nettie writes that as she left the farm, she was followed by Mr.____, who wanted to take advantage of her. Nettie manages to hurt Mr.____ just enough to escape. She finds her way to the home of the Reverend Mr.____, and is surprised to see a little girl with eyes just like her sister's open the door.

She is taken in by the reverend and his wife, Samuel and Corrine, and takes care of the children, Adam and Olivia. She finds happiness and friends within the family, but can't help but worry about Celie, who "laid [herself] down for me." Samuel and Corrine are missionaries who are preparing for work in Africa. Nettie becomes concerned when she doesn't get a response and understands that Mr.____ is keeping these letters from Celie. Nettie doesn't know what to do, since the family will leave for Africa soon and she will have to find a new job somewhere in town.

Later, Nettie writes with the news that she is going to Africa with Samuel and Corrine. One missionary canceled at the last minute because she suddenly was married, and Nettie was allowed to take the woman's place. As she prepares to leave, she goes into town for some things and meets Sofia, who is tending to the mayor's wife. Not knowing the history behind her, she writes to Celie that Sofia looked like "...the very last person in the world you'd expect to see waiting on anybody, and in particular not on anybody that looked like the mayor's wife."

She describes her trip to Africa by way of New York in vivid detail, everything surprising and delighting her. She reminds Celie that their ancestors were born in Africa, and that "millions and millions of Africans were captured and sold into slavery—you and me, Celie!" When she first sees the African coast, however, her soul vibrates "like a large bell." She wonders if she will ever be able to tell all to Celie.

Celie reads these letters in shock, unable to fight the urge to kill Mr.____ for what he has done. Shug pleads with her to keep her sanity because Nettie will return one day, and "she [would] be pissed if you change on her while she on her way home." Furthermore, if Celie kills Mr.____, then Shug will lose her. She doesn't want what happened with Sofia to happen with her. Celie asks Shug if she can sleep with her instead of Mr.____ while she is here, and Shug readily agrees.

Analysis

This section begins with a change of narration. A first-person narrative is still used, but it is from the perspective of another character. The impact of the text is different because Nettie is a more active participant in events than Celie. This can be seen in the only event shared by the two women, the contact that they both have with Sofia. Celie, earlier, could not offer any direct assistance in helping Sofia from jail. Nettie, however, talks to Sofia upon sight, and cannot believe that a woman like that could be in such a situation. The biggest difference between Nettie and Celie is that Nettie is active in dealing with her problems, while Celie has been mostly passive. This introduction of Nettie as a narrator is foreshadowing, or a clue that the text will now have a much more active voice.

The images of God and the church, which we have seen in symbols, are embodied in the characters of Corrine and Samuel. Earlier in the novel, the reader connected their possession of Olivia and Adam with the idea that they were protected, in a sense, by

God. Now that Nettie is within their family, she has also entered that sphere of protection. Yet when Nettie asks Samuel to check up on Celie and Mr.____, Samuel refuses to get involved, on the grounds that he "don't know them." Celie has not been protected, which is what we have known all along. She must fight for herself. This protection comes from within, and although Celie is kind and wonderful, the protection that she desires does not come from wishing for it. As Celie takes a more aggressive role, that protection, as well as true enlightenment, will come to her. But Samuel's refusal to get involved indicates that now is not the time.

Nettie still has her own trials and tribulations to endure, however, and the road to Africa is filled with symbols. As she heads toward Africa, the travel allows her to broaden her own perspective. She is a reliable narrator because she is humble yet intelligent. Her first instinct upon learning new things is to share them with her sister, so the letters of the journey are filled with wonder and discovery. The most significant knowledge is her self-knowledge as a black woman. She is very sensitive to how the blacks are treated in America (her trip on the train) and how other blacks treat her (the trip to Harlem and Senegal). Her questions on slavery indicate that she finds it hard to understand why black people around the world do not necessarily feel kinship with one another. The conflict of black vs. black makes no sense to her, even though she has experienced this very conflict within her own family. As she goes to Africa, these questions of slavery serve to foreshadow some possible unpleasantness they will find as missionaries. Samuel thinks that the missionaries and the Africans "are the same" and that they have "a common goal." This might be true, but suspense runs through this narrative as the missionaries prepare to meet the Olinka tribe.

Study Questions

1. Why does Nettie correct herself when she says that Corrine and Samuel have been "like family to me"?

2. Why does Nettie still write to Celie after she realizes that Mr.____ won't let her have these letters?

3. What does Nettie want to tell Corrine and Samuel about their children, who "were sent by God" to them?

4. When does Nettie come into contact with American prejudice?

5. How do the people of Harlem feel about Africa?

6. How do the so-called "Europeans" of the Missionary Society differ from the "Africans," according to Nettie?

7. What is the name of the ship that takes Nettie across the Atlantic?

8. List Nettie's itinerary from England to Africa.

9. What doesn't Nettie like about the Senegalese?

10. What did Christ want to add on to the end of the commandment, "Thou Shalt Not Kill," and why, according to Shug?

Answers

1. Nettie realizes that Samuel and Corrine have been kinder to her than her own family, so she says that they have been like her own family "might have been."

2. Nettie is very lonely, and she remembers that Celie still writes letters to God whenever she feels the need to write. Nettie takes Celie for inspiration and continues to send letters because it makes her feel better thinking that her sister might one day read them.

3. Nettie wants to tell them that "God has sent [Olivia and Adam] their sister and aunt."

4. Nettie, along with the entire family, had to sit in the "sit-down" section of the train, without beds. They were not allowed to use the restaurant, and had to use different toilets. In addition to this, when they meet a white man in South Carolina who asks them where they are going, he turns and says to his wife, "Niggers going to Africa, now I have seen everything."

5. The people in Harlem love Africa, and even the children contribute their pennies to the missionaries.

6. The "Europeans" or white missionaries were supposedly successful because they didn't "coddle their charges." Samuel points out that they have a different agenda from the previous missionaries. While the white missionaries wanted to educate the "savages" in order to spread the word of God, Samuel, Corrine, and Nettie are "black like the Africans themselves." Their goal is to work for "the uplift of black people everywhere."

7. The ship is called the Malaga.

8. Nettie leaves Southampton, England on July 24, and is scheduled to arrive in Monrovia, Liberia on September 12. There will be stops in Lisbon, Portugal, and Dakar, Senegal.

9. The Senegalese in the market were too concerned about selling their products, and Nettie felt that they looked through her "as quickly as...the French white people who lived there" if she didn't buy anything.

10. Shug thinks that Jesus Christ probably wanted to add "starting with me," because He realized there were fools in this world that good people would want to kill.

Suggested Essay Topics

1. What does England symbolize in this novel? Compare and contrast England and Africa and their effects upon Nettie.

2. Do you find Nettie's attitude (and the attitude of the missionaries) toward Africa condescending?

Letters 61-63

New Characters:

Joseph: *the guide of the missionaries*

Tashi: *a young Olinka girl and best friend of Olivia*

Tashi's mother (Catherine) and father: *the parents*

Summary

Celie starts to feel a little better now that she knows that Nettie is alive, but she still wonders about her children. Shug had told her that children that are born from an incestual relationship turn out to be "dunces."

After a long, difficult journey, the missionaries arrive at the Olinka village. The Olinkas are surprised that the new missionaries are black and that there are two women among them. Samuel is asked by the villagers if Corrine or Nettie is the mother of the children, and then asked if he has two wives. After Samuel tells them about himself and his family, the missionaries are invited to watch a special ceremony welcoming them. The greatest part of the ceremony is a dance and story which pays homage to the roofleaf, a thick plant which is abundant in the village and covers every hut.

Nettie is told a legend, in which a greedy chief starts to hoard all the crops and wives in the village. There was always an overabundance of crops, so there always seemed to be enough for everybody. However, when a storm blew away all of the roofs of the villages, they discovered, to their dismay, that there was no more roof leaf to cover their houses. Their village is almost wiped out during the rainy season. The greedy chief is banished from the village, and once the roofleaf is abundant again, the people worship and pay homage to the crops. Nettie wonders what Celie "will make of all this."

Nettie soon becomes adjusted to her daily routine, which involves a lot of work teaching the children and adults. Olivia is the only girl in these classes, since the Olinka do not believe in educating girls. In their system, a woman can strive only to be "the mother of [her husband's] children." Olivia wonders about her best friend, Tashi, and if she will be able to join her at school. They spend a lot of time together, which worries Tashi's parents, who fear that their daughter "knows she is learning a way of life she will never live." They ask Nettie to keep Tashi from seeing Olivia. When Nettie pleads that Tashi might become something more than the tribe expects of her, Tashi's father replies that "our people pity people such as [Nettie], who are cast out, into a world...where you must struggle all alone." Tashi will always have "someone to look after"

her, whether it is a husband or a father. Nettie is surprised that she "is an object of pity and contempt...to men and women alike" in the village.

As time passes, Corrine starts to change as well. She becomes jealous of Nettie because the tribe considers her to be Samuel's wife as well. First, she asks that the children not call her "Mama Nettie" anymore. Eventually, she asks her to stop borrowing clothes. Nettie is hurt by this and asks Corrine if she is feeling all right.

Analysis

The missionaries find out that they must adjust to a different social system in Africa. The oppression of women in Africa is just as obvious and distasteful to Nettie as it was in America. The differences in the social system in Africa seem to be cosmetic. While the bigamy is legally recognized here, Mr.____ and Harpo practice what is in effect bigamy in America. Women are generally considered second-class citizens in Africa, and their dreams and desires are suppressed to give men control. Walker has already established this sort of treatment in Celie's town. Walker now puts Nettie in the same sort of situation that Celie was in to establish the independence of Nettie's character. Nettie is a bit upset by these developments, but never stops believing that she is correct. While she is surprised that she is looked upon with pity in the village, she jokes about it to Celie, calling herself a "pitiful, cast-out woman who may perish during the rainy season." Her self-worth is not affected by this pity or this oppression, however, which is a marked contrast with Celie's reaction to her role.

This system plays a more significant role in the battle for Tashi. Tashi is a young girl who may become suppressed at an early age, and threatens to become the same type of girl that Celie became after being abused. While Celie's abuse is more overt, Tashi is also a victim of repression. Nettie sees that Tashi should not suffer from this inequity, and battles with her father over control. Nettie struggles to become the "savior" that Celie never had. However, Tashi's father believes that he is protecting his daughter (this symbol of protection can be found in the roofleaf). Everyone in the town looks after one another, but only at the price of restricting freedom. Nettie believes in the kindness of protecting one another but also believes that it can be done while allowing women to have freedom. She wants Tashi's gifts to be applied beyond the village. While the Olinka women lead sheltered lives, they treat the men like little boys, giving them whatever they wish. As we have already learned from Celie's relationship with Mr.____, such protection can hardly be worth the lives that these women lead.

This system does have a profound effect upon Corrine and her relationship with Nettie. If there is a difference between these two systems it is that all women in the Olinka tribe are equal, and below men. Corrine, who enjoyed a superior role in America, now realizes that her worth is limited to that of her husband. Since Nettie is another woman who comes to Africa with Samuel, the villagers treat her as they do Corrine. This is something that Corrine finds difficult, since her role as wife to Samuel and mother to their children is belittled by Nettie's presumed sharing of this role. Corrine tries to keep Nettie down by reminding her that she borrowed her clothes and refusing to let their children call her "Mama Nettie." Corrine feels that this removal of symbols will cause her to be lowered in the eyes of the villagers. Corrine's jealousy comes from the villagers' perception, however, and because these are American symbols of value, all that is accomplished is the wounding of Nettie's feelings. Corrine deals with the town's perception by battling Nettie, when her anger should be directed at the town for possessing such a perception.

Study Questions

1. What does Celie learn about the weather in Africa?
2. Describe Joseph, the guide and translator.
3. What does Nettie notice about the Africans' teeth?
4. How does Nettie describe the jungle?
5. What happened to the white missionary who was at the Olinka village?
6. What food is served at the welcoming ceremony?
7. Describe Nettie's daily routine.
8. How is Olivia treated at school?
9. What does Tashi's father want Nettie to do?

10. Why does the way Olinka men speak to women remind Nettie of Pa?

Answers

1. Celie learns that it is "hot like cooking dinner on a big stove in a little kitchen in August and July" in Africa.

2. Joseph is short, fat, and soft, "with hands that seem not to have any bones in them." He is also "a deep chocolate brown."

3. Nettie is surprised that the Africans all have perfect, white teeth.

4. Nettie says the jungle is "trees and trees and then more trees on top of that. And vines. And ferns. And little animals."

5. The Olinka buried the last missionary one year ago.

6. They are given a chicken-and-peanut stew, which they eat with their fingers, and palm wine.

7. Nettie wakes up at five o'clock for a light breakfast and morning classes. They stop at eleven o'clock for lunch and household duties. From one to four o'clock it "is too hot to move," and then she teaches adult classes at five o'clock.

8. She is the only girl at school, and only her brother, Adam, talks to her.

9. Tashi's father wants Nettie to continue teaching, but only to the male children.

10. There is a total lack of interest in and respect for what Olinka women have to say. An Olinka woman cannot even look at a man's face while talking. Nettie writes that the way Olinka women behave around men is "our own behavior around Pa."

Suggested Essay Topics

1. How does the difference in setting contribute to the atmosphere of Nettie's story? Compare and contrast symbols of weather and climate with those that exist in Celie's story.

2. How does the story of the roofleaf establish the plant as a symbol of protection? Analyze the legend.

Letters 64–69

New Character:

Daisy: *Alphonso's new wife*

Summary

Five years have passed between letters as Nettie picks up her narrative. Tashi's father died in the rainy season the year before, and Catherine, Tashi's mother, insists that her daughter continue to learn. As the years go by, Tashi becomes a wonderful storyteller and cries when she hears about slavery, which is something the other villagers refuse to acknowledge. Other women begin to send their daughters to school as well, which is reluctantly accepted by the men.

Corrine tells Nettie not to come to their hut if Samuel is alone. Nettie complains that "since Corrine almost never visits me herself I will hardly have anybody to talk to, just in friendship." Corrine thinks that the other villagers "get the wrong idea," even though it seems that most of the villagers are preoccupied with the road that is finally being built near the Olinka village.

As the road approaches the village, the people of the Olinka tribe are happy that there will finally be an easy way to get to the coast. Nettie talks of an exciting celebration and barbecue that will take place as soon as the road gets to the town. The next letter, however, is written a year later, and Nettie picks up the story with the disturbing news that the road was designed to go through the village rather than to the village. When the chief of the Olinka tribe travels to the coast, he discovers many more displaced Africans and learns that the entire area has been bought by a British rubber company. The tribe now must pay a tax for their own water and rent for their own village. Even though the tribe laughs at first, it becomes clear that it is not a joke.

Corrine falls ill with African fever, and as she becomes sicker and sicker, her jealousy and hatred of Nettie grows. She believes that Nettie is the mother of Adam and Olivia, and that she had them with Samuel in America. Nettie and Samuel swear on a Bible that this is not true, but Corrine is not convinced. Samuel then con-fides to Nettie that the reason he took her in was because he also thought that she was the mother of Adam and Olivia. Upon hear-ing this, Nettie asks Samuel to tell her how they found the chil-dren.

Samuel tells her the following story. The children were brought to him by an old friend, a "scamp," who claims that these were the last children of his wife. He had married his wife when she was weak from the shock of the lynching of her first husband. She had two children from this first husband, Celie and Nettie. When Samuel first saw Nettie, however, she looked so much like the chil-dren that Samuel figured his friend was lying and actually had the children with her. Nettie realizes that his old friend is Alphonso, the man Celie and Nettie thought was their father, and that their actual father died before they knew him.

Celie, after reading this letter, is shocked. She learns that her "pa is not pa" and that all the other things she had thought about herself are not true. She tells God "you must be sleep" and Shug tells her to come to Memphis with her and Grady.

Celie feels the need to meet her "father" again, however, and she travels with Shug to see him. She finds out that he has a new wife and even more children. She tells him about Nettie and what she knows, but he doesn't really care. He tells her that her real fa-ther "didn't know how to git along" with whites, which is why he was lynched. He can tell that Shug knows about what he did to Celie but really doesn't care. Celie wants to know where her par-ents are buried, but Alphonso replies that it was an unmarked grave. With no tombstone to mark her parents, Celie is kissed by Shug, who tells her that "us each other's peoples now."

Analysis

In this section of the novel, the stability of Nettie's and Celie's lives is destroyed by events beyond their control. The destruction of the Olinka village is followed by the rift in Corrine's and Nettie's friendship. Progress and the process of change play important roles in this section.

Progress is symbolized by the road, which the Olinka naively believe is there for them. Nettie is surprised that the town believes

that it is the center of the universe and that everything that is done is done for it. This progress cuts through the village right through the middle, and has a humbling effect upon the town. The town never had to deal with a force so strong, and finds itself unable to deal with rapid change. This reflects the town's reaction to having girls study for the first time. This idea is foreign to them, and they are unable to deal with rapid changes in ideas. Because they are so used to stability and the comfort of tradition, they end up in shock when these traditions are quickly cast away. This betrayal is hard for the people to accept because they have never been betrayed before. Celie has been able to deal with heartache because she has hardly experienced anything except broken promises, and now expects to be disappointed. The Olinka tribe must deal with the fact that they have been betrayed, in addition to the betrayal itself. While Celie found solace in prayer, the tribe can do nothing but pretend that everything is fine. Ironically, the tribe's denial is as effective as Celie's prayer.

The Olinka react as a society to mistreatment in the same way Celie has always acted. Celie became unable to fight back because she found this abuse overwhelming, just as the Olinka people find the fact that their land was bought from under them overwhelming. Nettie's revelation that their father is actually not their father turns the uncomfortable peace that Celie has made with her life on its head. Celie throws up her hands and finally gives up on God. This reaction is a result of all of this suppression of her feelings; she had continued to turn to God with her problems and was ignored. Her blasphemy and dismissal of God is extreme behavior but justifiable since she feels so betrayed. She has, at last, learned that the solution to her problems lies within herself. She acts by visiting her "father" to find out where her real father is buried. She also searches for her father's grave and reaffirms her friendship with Shug. These are all things that she can now do because this crisis has forced her out of her shell. She no longer acts like "an ostrich," which is precisely the way the Olinka people now behave.

Corrine exhibits this same sort of ostrich-like behavior by continually harassing Nettie. Her cruel behavior comes from fear that she is living a lie as Nettie and Celie were. The irony is that this is not the case (we already know that Celie is the children's mother, not Nettie), but to Samuel and Corrine, the answer is clear. Corrine was supposedly protected by God, but this fear has caused her to lose faith in God. Nettie's swearing on a Bible doesn't convince her that Nettie is telling the truth.

Walker uses the "sickness" that Corrine suffers as a metaphor for pettiness and refusal to support her "sister." The African sickness that Corrine suffers from is not only physical; she also exhibits jealous behavior that mirrors the pettiness of the Olinka men. However, being a woman, Corrine does not possess the power to get rid of her nemesis. As a result, she becomes even more frustrated, and she is convinced that the other members of the family are conspiring to keep a secret from her. While the other women of this novel have tried to support one another, Corrine feels that she must vanquish another woman in order to assume her proper role as mother to Adam and Olivia. In acting this way, she only makes herself "sicker."

Study Questions

1. Why is Nettie proud of the villagers as they talk with the roadbuilders?

2. How have Adam and Olivia changed during their five years in Africa?

3. Describe an Olinka funeral.

4. How is Samuel made uneasy by the relationships between men and women in the Olinka village?

5. What does Nettie mean when she says "a grown child is a dangerous thing"?

6. How does Corrine treat the children now?

7. Why does Corrine want to examine Nettie's stomach?

8. How did Celie's mother become mentally unstable after her first husband died, according to the story?

9. What is the "key" to handling white people, according to Alphonso?

10. Why doesn't Celie's father have a marked grave?

Answers

1. Nettie is proud of the people of the Olinka tribe because they always show up with foods and gifts for the roadbuilders, proving that they are a generous and loving tribe.

2. Adam and Olivia are almost as tall as Nettie now. Both have learned so much that Adam is afraid that there will be nothing left for Samuel to teach.

3. The women of the village paint their faces white and wear white shrouds. While they "cry in a high keening voice" the body is wrapped in barkcloth and buried.

4. Samuel's job is "to preach the Bible's directive of one husband and one wife." He is also confused because the women of the village seem happy and always spend time with one another. They do it in order to keep away from their husbands, not because they are happy with their lives.

5. The Olinka men are "children" because they are spoiled by their wives. They act irrationally, are overly sensitive, and do not understand the consequences of their actions. Nettie feels that this childish behavior is dangerous because Olinka men possess the power of life and death over their wives. A wife can be killed if her husband simply accuses her of witchcraft. This power, coupled with immaturity, makes for a dangerous person.

6. Corrine can't bear to look at the children; she hadn't even told them that they were adopted.

7. She thinks there are stretch marks on Nettie's stomach, which would prove that she was the mother of Olivia and Adam.

8. Celie's mother continued to act as if her husband was alive, and set his place at the table. She would also tell her neighbors grandiose plans for the future that she was making with her husband.

9. Alphonso always believed that the key to handling whites was money. Celie's father was killed because he never gave money to the whites, supposedly, and Alphonso makes it a point to hire a white boy in his store and "just right off offer to give him money."

10. Celie's father was lynched, and lynch mobs do not provide crosses or headstones for their victims.

Suggested Essay Topics

1. How has Celie's "father" changed over the years? Do you feel that his cruelty has gone unpunished? Use examples from the text to support your decision.

2. How do the villagers react to the stories about slavery? What does this imply about the villagers?

Letters 70–73

Summary

Nettie tells Samuel and Corrine that she is the aunt of Adam and Olivia, and her sister, Celie, is their mother. Corrine, however, doesn't believe her. Nettie tries to make Corrine remember her meeting with Celie in the dry goods store years ago, but Corrine doesn't remember. When Nettie shows her a quilt made from the cloth that Corrine had bought so long ago in order to make Olivia a dress, Corrine starts to cry. She had blocked Celie out of her memory because she looked so much like Olivia that Corrine was afraid that Celie would want her daughter back. Samuel, Corrine, and Nettie hold each other until Corrine drifts off to sleep. Later, she murmurs to Samuel, "I believe," and dies.

Corrine is buried in the Olinka way, and everyone suffers from her loss. Samuel, especially, seems "like someone lost." Nettie takes this moment of loss to lament for Celie and pray that she eventually meets with her sister. Samuel asks Nettie to describe Celie, and Nettie is so anxious to tell someone about her sister that her words "pour out like water." Samuel regrets that he did not interfere in Celie's marriage with Mr.____.

Celie, meanwhile, addresses her new letter to Nettie, not God. She pretends not to know God, which shocks and offends Shug. Celie is surprised to hear that Shug believes in God, considering the life she has led. Shug, however, tells Celie that God is inside you, and not in the church. Shug does not believe in Christianity; to her, God is in everything and the true way to love and worship God is to appreciate what God has made. Celie tries hard to "chase that old white man," the stereotypical image of God, out of her mind. She tries to accept the belief that "God is everything" and to learn to love God in a spiritual manner. However, she finds this "hard work"; she has thought that God was a white man her entire life. Now that she wants to forget this man, "he don't want to budge."

Analysis

In the previous section, Corrine and Celie both suffered crises that affected their entire lives. Now, they both begin a long healing process. Celie and Corrine must learn to live their lives despite the crises and to trust others again. Fortunately, even though they have lost their faith, they have not lost the people who love and support them. Walker uses this section not only to present the conflicts of two women who have crises of faith, but to introduce into the novel concepts of faith and religion removed from standard Christianity. Walker had discarded Christianity long before she wrote her first novel, and the ideas introduced in this section parallel her own beliefs, which are based upon nature and African folklore.

Corrine doesn't believe anything anymore, even though Nettie has let her see her stomach to prove she wasn't pregnant. It is easier for Corrine to believe that it is possible to "rub out" stretch marks. Nettie is able to jog Corrine's memory by using the quilt, which Walker uses as a symbol of protection in this novel. By bringing Corrine the quilt and showing her the fabric, Corrine is able to re-member Celie. Symbolically, Nettie "laid the quilt across the bed," covering Corrine, and in effect, giving her the support she needs. Corrine is fully healed when she holds on to Samuel and Nettie, fixing the circle that had been broken. Having done this, Corrine can die in peace.

Celie's blasphemy is not so easy to fix, since it has been brought about by years of unanswered prayer. The reader is surprised to find out that Shug becomes a symbol of spirituality, since her behavior has never been stereotypically holy. Her reasoning,

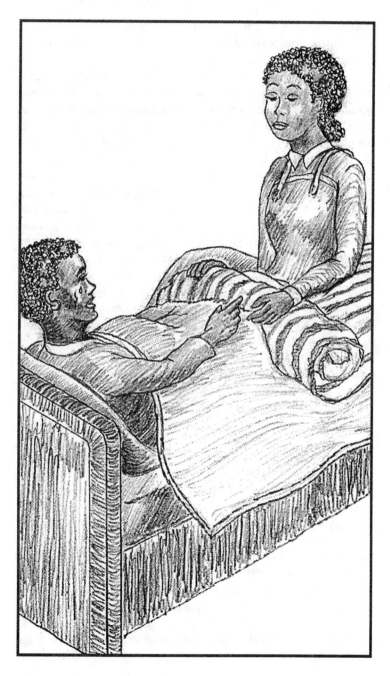

however, does explain why Celie's prayers have gone unanswered, and why the church has been the scene of some horrible acts committed against women.

Shug has been a sensual person, and her talk of "devil's music" implied that she was immoral, but that was only because the church-goers equated sex with immorality. Shug has never felt this way, and explains to Celie that God is a force rather than a person, and church is a place where people go to share God, not find God. Since most of the people in their church are part of a society that treats women shamefully, Celie points out that there is not much of God to share within the church. God should be worshipped through enjoying what it creates, says Shug, which means that even sex should be enjoyed, since it was a creation of God. Once one sees this, "you can just relax, go with everything that's going, and praise God by liking what you like." Celie, however, is used to being guilty about her feelings and having her prayers go unanswered. Nevertheless, she wants to be able to love God. Since she can no longer tolerate the old God, she will push herself to accept this new doctrine.

What Celie finds hardest to accept is Shug's belief that kindness can be done to God simply by appreciating the creations that are made. Shug tells Celie that she believes "it pisses God off if you walk by the color purple in a field somewhere and don't even notice it." The significance of the color purple goes back to one of the first sections of the novel, when Celie wanted a purple dress but chose a blue one because Mr.____ would not have paid for a purple one. At the time, the color of the dress was simply an element of control, a way of showing that Mr.____ forced Celie to accept his choices. Now, with the color chosen by Shug as one of God's favorite creations, it also is a symbol of this spirituality, of the love of God without needless worship. Celie, in fact, had wanted this from the very beginning, only to be oppressed by her husband. Her choice of purple embodied her desire for the spirituality and love that came from this color, the spirituality and love from a God she could recognize. Now that this love is open to her, after listening to Shug, Celie discovers that she has been so beaten with the image of God as a white man that she cannot immediately accept this.

The theme of faith, which has occurred often in this novel, now returns in a different setting, as the characters try to recover their lost faith. Corrine's recovery is easier because she is a woman who had lived with faith but temporarily lost it. Once she stops lying to herself and admits that she had seen Celie, she forgives and is forgiven, and once more returns to faith. Corrine's battle with jealousy causes her to discard her old system of values and beliefs, and accept the love of others. Her resentment was not limited to Nettie; she had always resented the Olinka tribe as well. Her reconciliation with Nettie, however, is symbolic of her inner peace, and the fact that she is buried in the Olinka way, rather than in the Christian way, illustrates the acceptance of her new faith. Celie has to learn real faith; she had never believed in any sort of God because her only image of God was a white man. Even though she had always prayed, it was easy for her to believe that the prayers went unanswered. Her life never improved, and she thought it was because she "knew white people never listened to colored, period." For her, accepting true faith is hard because she is still wary from following a faith in which she had never believed at all.

Study Questions

1. When Nettie tells Samuel and Corrine the entire story about Celie, what shocks Samuel the most?

2. What did the dry goods store smell like on the day Celie and Corrine met?

3. What does Corrine mean when she says to Nettie, "Don't touch my things. I'm not dead yet"?

4. What did Corrine remember about the clerk at the dry goods store?

5. From what college did Corrine graduate?

6. What do the villagers think about women who menstruate?

7. What is Celie's description of God?

8. Is God a man or woman, according to Shug?

9. Why doesn't God think that sex is dirty according to Shug?

10. What does Shug think about people who always try to please God?

Answers

1. Samuel is shocked that Celie was raped by her "father."

2. The dry goods store smelled like peanut shells.

3. Corrine thinks that Nettie is cheating her husband, and now wants to take her things as well. Corrine wants to remind her that she is still Samuel's wife.

4. Corrine was upset that the clerk treated her "like any other nigger."

5. Corrine graduated from Spelman Seminary.

6. Nettie writes that villagers "...think women who have their friends should not even be seen."

7. God is "big and old and tall and graybearded and white." Celie also says that "he wear white robes and go barefooted."

8. Shug says that "God ain't a he or a she, but an It."

9. Sex cannot be dirty because God made it, according to Shug.

10. According to Shug, the people that worry the most about pleasing God never see God "always trying to please us back."

Suggested Essay Topics

1. Nettie writes to Celie saying that there is a verse in the Bible which says that Jesus Christ has hair like "lamb's wool." Where is this passage in the Bible? Could you find other evidence in the Bible that God is not the stereotype invented by whites?

2. Has Shug always lived her life according to the philosophy that she explains to Celie? Find examples from the text to support your conclusions.

Letters 74–77

New Characters:

Jolentha (Suzie Q): *the little daughter of Squeak and Harpo*

Henrietta: *the little daughter of Sofia*

Jerene and Darlene: *twins who help Celie with her sewing*

Summary

Sofia is released from the mayor's house after serving eleven and a half years of a twelve-year sentence. To celebrate, everyone goes to Odessa's house for a dinner. At this dinner, Shug and Grady announce that they are returning to Memphis. Everyone, especially Mr.____, is disappointed when they hear this news, but that disappointment turns to shock when Shug announces that Celie is coming to Memphis as well. Mr.____ starts to protest, and Celie confronts him about hiding Nettie's letters and abusing her. No one can speak from the surprise of hearing Celie stand up for herself. Shug then announces that another person will come with them as well. Everyone thinks that this person is Sofia, but Sofia tells everybody that her home is with Odessa and Jack and her children. At that moment, however, Eleanor Jane comes to the door to ask Sofia for help. Sofia leaves with her. Squeak then announces that she wants to sing professionally, and will go to Memphis too. Squeak asks Sofia to take care of Harpo while she is gone.

As they prepare to leave, Mr.____ tells Celie that she won't be able to survive on her own because she is "black," "pore," "ugly," and "a woman." Celie feels a surge of energy run through her and tells Mr.____ that "until [he does] right by" her, "everything [he does] will fail."

As they travel up to Memphis, Grady tries to be as close to Squeak as possible. When they arrive in Memphis, Shug gives Celie a bedroom in her house. Celie is unsure about what she wants to do. While she thinks about her future plans, she continues to sew pairs of pants for Shug to wear on stage. When Celie finally makes the "perfect pair of pants," Shug spends her time looking in the

mirror and showing off to everybody. Squeak asks Celie if she can have a pair. Soon, all of her friends want pants and Shug tells Celie to put an advertisement in the paper. Celie signs her letter to Nettie as the head of her new company, "Folkspants, Unlimited."

Analysis

Celie's argument with Mr.___ is the climax of the novel. It is also the moment of the text that the reader has been waiting for. This is one of the most dramatic scenes in modern American literature, and also one of the funniest. Mr.___ and Harpo are revealed as nothing more than ineffectual buffoons, whose only power came from manipulating women too scared to fight back. Now that Celie has fought back, she seems to be unstoppable.

Because of Celie's declaration of freedom, the relationships between men and women have been permanently changed. Harpo is completely emasculated by Squeak's departure and Sofia's revelation that he is not the father of Henrietta. Harpo had attempted to use the same devices of control that he had employed while he was married to these women, but he is outdone by both women so badly that he has nothing left to say. He refers to Mary Agnes by the nickname, Squeak, and is quickly quieted, indicating that Mary Agnes wants nothing more to do with his derision and suppression. Mr.___ is forgotten by the rest of the group. When he does finally lash out at Celie, just as she is ready to leave for Memphis, he sounds like a little child throwing a tantrum. Celie replies with words that she says "come from the trees." With her new perspective of God, she seems to have answered her own prayers. Celie's friends, along with Celie's new faith, have given her the strength to fight back and the guidance with which to use this strength.

This strength and guidance is symbolized in the pants that she makes for everybody. The clothes that have been made in this story have always been symbols of protection; the women of this novel make dresses and quilts out of love. Celie now makes pants for everybody who wants them. It seems to her as if she cannot stop making them. Her pants make Shug feel "totally comfortable" and look wonderful even though she gets "bloated" from eating on the road. These pants seem to transform whoever wears them into goddesses and gods. Even though Celie makes these pants for men and women, the pants are especially important for the power that they give to the female characters. Pants are usually considered men's clothes, and are symbols of authority and power. We refer to the head of a household as the one "who wears the pants in the family." The fact that Celie can give this power to both men and women indicates that her world has dramatically changed. Celie is able to make gender meaningless by loving all. Now that she finally feels that she has power and faith, she wants to spread her love and protection to all the people in the world. The fact that her company is "Unlimited," rather than "Ltd.," implies that her love and protection is infinite.

Celie has made a grand transition, from a victim who had always needed help to one who can provide it to the needy. Celie makes a pair of red and purple pants for Sofia (red and purple were the colors that Celie wanted when Kate bought her a dress), hoping that these pants will help Sofia "jump over the moon" and protect her from her continued problems with Eleanor Jane. She also plans to make a pair of pants for Nettie, with which her sister will be protected from anything that can harm her in Africa. She tells Nettie that "every stitch I sew will be a kiss." All of her pants have been made by love and care, and every pair of pants that is worn is in effect, sewn by Celie's kisses. Now that she is aware of the power that she possesses, she looks to help others as she once was helped.

Study Questions

1. Who is "Mama" to Sofia's children?

2. What is the "welcome mat" that Celie is going to use to "enter Creation"?

3. What is wrong with Miss Eleanor's family?

4. Why must Sofia "act nice"?

5. What is the curse that Celie puts on Mr.____?

6. Why does Shug give Celie a bedroom in the back of the house?

7. What kind of pants does Mary Agnes pick out for herself?

8. Describe how Celie designs a pair of pants for Jack.

9. Does Celie care about Darlene's teaching her to speak correctly?

10. What does Shug feel about Celie's speech?

Answers

1. Sofia's younger children call Odessa "Mama" and Sofia "Miss Sofia."

2. Celie wants to use Mr.____'s dead body symbolically to "enter Creation," since leaving him would be the same to her as entering the Kingdom of Heaven.

3. Jack tells the entire group that there is a lot of drinking in the mayor's family and that the son (presumably Billy) has had trouble in college.

4. Sofia is still on parole and doesn't want to end up back in jail.

5. Celie tells Mr.____ that everything that he has done to her is "already done to" him, and everything that he plans to do will come back to haunt him.

6. Shug knows that Celie likes to wake up with the sun on her face.

7. She picks a pair that is "the color of sunset, orangish with a little grayish fleck."

8. Celie makes Jack's pants with big pockets so that he can hold "little children's things," such as marbles and rocks. She decides to make narrow legs so that Jack will be able to run in case a child gets in trouble. She makes them "something he can lay back in when he hold Odessa in front of the fire."

9. Celie doesn't care because she is happy now.

10. Shug says that Celie "can talk in sign language for all I care."

Suggested Essay Topics

1. Look back at how Shug and Celie describe their dream house, and the purpose of designing such a house.

2. What is the relationship between Sofia and Eleanor Jane based upon? Can you predict how this relationship will end?

Letters 78–79

Summary

Hearing that Sofia's mother died, Celie comes back to pay a visit to Harpo and Sofia. She has changed so much that Mr.____ doesn't even recognize her as she walks across his farm. As she approaches their house, Celie can hear Harpo and Sofia fighting. Sofia intends to be a pallbearer at her mother's funeral but Harpo thinks that "peoples use to men doing this sort of thing." Sofia is adamant, and during a lull in their argument Celie knocks on the door. They both stop everything and greet Celie warmly.

Harpo wants to know why Mary Agnes acts so detached, and Celie tells him that she has been constantly smoking marijuana. Grady grows and sells marijuana from his backyard, and Celie shares a cigarette with Sofia and Harpo.

At the funeral, Sofia and her sisters look like "amazons." They march in carrying the coffin, and the other mourners "act like this is the way it always done." After the funeral, Celie notices how clean Mr.____ looks. Mr.____ comes up to Celie and talks politely, but is clearly afraid of her. He tells her that Henrietta, Sofia's youngest daughter, has a blood disease and might die soon. He is concerned about Sofia. She has already lost her mother and losing her daughter would cause her even greater suffering.

After he leaves, Sofia tells Celie that Mr.____ was a wreck after she left him. He lived "like a pig" and refused to take care of himself. It was Harpo who cleaned and fed him because Mr.____ was "too gone to care." Sofia says that she fell in love with Harpo again when she saw him holding his father in his arms while he was sleeping. Mr.____ started to improve after Harpo forced him to give Celie the rest of her letters from Nettie, prompting Sofia to say "you know [that] meanness kill."

Analysis

Celie returns to Mr.____'s farm a changed woman, to the point that Mr.____ doesn't even recognize her. Her dramatic change in appearance reflects her change of character, but it also shows that

Mr.____ had never looked at Celie as a woman, which is why it is hard for him to recognize her now. Celie walks by in full regalia, including the pants that she made for herself. She is dressed, literally and symbolically, as an empowered woman. She shows a bit of her power when she convinces Harpo and Sofia to try marijuana; both of them hear something that they had never heard before when they try the cigarette. It sounds to them like "everything," indicating that they are in contact with something more powerful than they have usually experienced. They are able to have this contact because Celie is there with them.

However, when she gets to Harpo's and Sofia's house, it sounds as if Harpo is up to his old tricks again. Harpo does not want her to be a pallbearer because he considers it men's work. Harpo tried to force his ideas upon his wives because he believed, from watching Mr.____, that it was normal for him to do so. Now society dictates the social rules, and no one has a problem with Sofia and her sisters doing this work. This causes Celie to exult that she loves "folks," because they have now become smart enough to let women do what they desire. Harpo's ideas have now become anachronistic, and his chauvinism is powerless.

Celie uses marijuana to help Sofia and Harpo understand how she feels and what this transition in her life has meant to her. Alice Walker has been an advocate of marijuana, and her views are embodied in Celie's philosophy of its use. Celie differentiates her occasional use from Grady's and Squeak's abuse of the drug. Just as Walker and Zora Neale Hurston felt that occasional use stimulated creativity, Celie uses it only when she wants to "feel closer to God." Now, she feels so wonderful she doesn't need it, but Celie decries the overuse of Grady and Squeak, which has left them "feeble-minded." When Harpo, Sofia, and Celie smoke, they hear a humming that they had never experienced before, which Celie believes to be "everything." This experience is a physical sensation similar to Shug's philosophy of God's presence. The scene illustrates the wider range of life that Celie has experienced. Celie had constantly prayed without once feeling close to God; now she "makes love" to God almost every day.

Despite her wider vision, Celie nevertheless expects Mr.____ to still follow his chauvinistic beliefs. However, he seems to have dramatically improved in character and appearance. Even though Mr.____ is devastated by the loss of his wife, this loss causes him to become vulnerable. Once he is vulnerable, his unhappy life of dominating weak women ends. So, surprisingly, Celie walking out on Mr.____ is the best thing to happen to him and his son, because it creates a situation in which the men must rely on themselves. This allows them to help one another, and be concerned with their own personal development. It was the same type of situation that brought Shug and Celie together, which led to their friendship and support of one another. The symbolic act of holding his father while sleeping makes Harpo the same type of protector that Celie and Shug were to each other. This change is reflected in the cleaned-up house and the now-working Mr.____. Celie was only a servant to Mr.____ and Harpo, she never could do anything out of love because she didn't love them. Celie's departure forces Harpo to love his father, out of fear for his death at first, then because he truly cares. The relationship between Harpo and his father, which has always been based upon intimidation, is now based on love. As a result of this love, Mr.____ can now show affection to others, and demonstrates this by returning Celie's letters. Even though Celie is understandably wary, the reader begins to wonder if even Mr.____ can change his ways.

Study Questions

1. How is Harpo's and Sofia's house different from before?

2. What will Sofia's sisters look like as pallbearers, according to Harpo? What is Sofia's reply?

3. Why must Sofia always have things her own way?

4. How much does one of Grady's cigarettes cost?

5. Why is marijuana like whiskey, according to Celie?

6. How does Celie reply when Sofia tells her that Mr.____ is "trying to git religion"?

7. What does Mr.____ say about Sofia's mother?

8. What does Celie try to remember about Nettie's letters?

9. What was Mr.____ most scared of when he slept alone?

10. Is it easy for Sofia to live with Harpo now?

Answers

1. The new house is bigger, away from the juke joint.

2. Harpo thinks that the three sisters will look like "they ought to be home frying chicken." Sofia replies that since her three brothers will carry the other side of the coffin, they will "look like field hands."

3. Sofia's mother had said a long time ago that Sofia thinks her way is as good as anyone else's.

4. Grady sells his marijuana cigarettes for a dime each.

5. A little drink of whiskey doesn't bother anyone, but "when you can't git started without asking the bottle, you in trouble." Marijuana is the same way to Celie; smoking it once in a while doesn't bother her.

6. Celie thinks that a "devil" like Mr.____ can try to become religious, but it doesn't mean that he will succeed. Celie jokes that "trying is bout all he can do."

7. Mr.____ says that "the woman that brought Sofia in the world brought something."

8. Celie seems to remember that Nettie had written about a cure for the disease that Henrietta suffers from that is used in Africa.

9. Mr.____ couldn't bear to hear the sound of his own heart, which was at times as loud as "drums."

10. Sofia is the first to admit that living with Harpo hasn't been easy, but nevertheless, she started "to feel again for Harpo."

Suggested Essay Topics

1. What does Mr.____ realize as he sleeps alone and hears his own heartbeat?

2. Why do Grady and Squeak continually smoke "reefer," and how does this affect their characters?

Letters 80–81

New Characters:

Doris Baines: *an old missionary from England*

Harold: *a small African child, and the adopted grandson of Doris Baines*

Althea: *Samuel's aunt, a missionary*

Theodosia: *Corrine's aunt, a missionary and friend to Althea*

Edward DuBoyce: *a young Harvard scholar*

Summary

Nettie begins her letter by announcing that she and Samuel were married the previous fall. They were married in England, where they tried to get some help for the Olinkas. The entire village was displaced in order to build new headquarters for the rubber plantation. All of the huts are destroyed and the villagers must live in a gigantic shelter, covered in tin, which had to be paid for by the villagers themselves. Samuel and Nettie feel powerless to stop this and decide that they must go to England in order to receive some justice.

On their way to England, they meet Doris Baines, a wealthy former missionary who writes novels and travels with a small African child she has adopted as a grandson.

Having been born wealthy, Doris is dreadfully bored and decides to become a missionary in order to live in an isolated environment. She was sent to Africa. Using the family fortune, she builds up an entire town by herself. The chief of the tribe is so grateful that he sends her a couple of women as wives, since he doesn't believe that she is a woman. Doris educates the girls and gives them to a couple of local men. She now enjoys being the "grandmama" of their children.

Once the group arrives in England, the Missionary Society is more interested in finding out why Nettie didn't leave as soon as Corrine died, so that "appearances" could be kept up and the natives wouldn't get the wrong idea. The problems of the Olinka are

not even discussed, and Samuel and Nettie leave disgusted. Samuel feels that there is nothing left to do except encourage the Olinka tribe to join the mbeles, the renegades who live in the forest, apart from the white men.

While Nettie and Samuel spend time together in England, Samuel tells Nettie about how he had met Corrine. Samuel's aunt and Corrine's aunt were good friends, and they would bombard Samuel and Corrine with incessant stories of their adventures. The young lovers take these stories from their aunts with good humor. One night, Corrine's aunt begins an often-heard tale of how she received an award from King Leopold of Belgium, when a young scholar interrupts her with tales of King Leopold's cruelty. Samuel now understands Theodosia's feelings, because he too feels un-appreciated for all the effort that he put in trying to improve the Olinka village. Nettie tries to comfort Samuel, and in doing so, the comfort turns to passion for one another.

Once they announce to the children their plans to marry, Samuel and Nettie tell Adam and Olivia about their real mother. Adam is disturbed to hear that Celie is an abused wife, but Samuel promises that they will return to America soon and find her. After they are married, however, Olivia tells Nettie about something else which is bothering Adam. He is in love with Tashi, and concerned for her because she is about to have her face scarred, which is part of a coming-of-age ritual. What is worse, however, is that Tashi will undergo female circumcision, which is also part of the initiation ceremony.

When they return to the Olinka village, Adam and Olivia search for Tashi but cannot find her. She is missing for two days, but then returns to the village in pain from the scars around her face. Adam turns his back on Tashi after seeing the scars, and wishes to return to America. Nettie is hopeful that Adam will forgive Tashi. She has to work harder than ever in order to keep the village alive, but she is happier because she now has "a loving soul to share [her life] with."

Analysis

Nettie and Samuel try to hinder the force of progress from destroying the Olinka village, but all hope seems to be vanishing.

The loss of roofleaf, the symbol of protection by God, to man-made tin embodies the uglier side of progress. The fact that the road and the rubber plants are being built for an upcoming war symbolizes the negative side of progress as well. As a result, Nettie and Samuel seem powerless to help. Once they realize that they cannot help, they understand that they have not been helping from the very beginning.

This understanding comes from meeting Doris Baines, a truly successful missionary. Her success comes, ironically, from not caring; if she wasn't born into vast wealth she could never have helped the Akweans. She helps only because she wants to be alone, and she invests absolutely no time personally. This is one of the few times Walker points out the division of races in this society; a white woman has the money to get this job done but nothing else, while the black missionaries have the desire and the dreams but no one has faith in them to give them the necessary resources. Doris Baines is an example of what the black women in this novel could be if they only weren't stymied by poverty. If Doris can accomplish so much with only money, so much that the chief doesn't even realize that Doris is a woman, imagine what Nettie could have done with the same amount of money and her spirit. Doris is rewarded with her solitude and grandchildren, symbols that imply that she has the fun without any of the responsibility. Samuel and Nettie, on the other hand, seem horribly burdened by responsibility.

It is this burden that causes them to lose faith in themselves. Samuel breaks down when he experiences this crisis, because he had worked all his life toward achieving the goal of making a difference in Africa. His anecdote about Corrine's aunt chillingly illustrates this dilemma. Theodosia is a bore, but only because her adventures are over and she wants to be recognized for her accomplishments. Instead, she is called a de facto supporter of a murderous regime by a young hothead.

Samuel has devoted his life to the church, but nonetheless has a personal need, like we all do, to feel recognized for what he has done. Instead, it becomes harder for him as he is less appreciated by the next generation. Nettie points out that they weren't asked to come, but Samuel replies that they are hardly even noticed. There is a wide bridge between the missionaries and the Olinka, and Samuel feels like a failure because he hasn't been able to bridge the gap and only now admits this to himself. The only person who could see this gap was Corrine, and "her awareness fueled [her] sickness." Unfortunately, Samuel is so distraught that he misses the way he has affected the lives of people, such as Tashi and Catherine.

However, this crisis does have one positive effect: it allows Nettie, in the guise of giving comfort, to love Samuel. Not unlike the situation involving Harpo and Mr.____ previously, once Samuel feels her love he naturally wants to reciprocate, and as a result, a new unit of support is formed. Walker is using this personal relationship to show how an individual can affect the life of another individual. Samuel is, of course, heartbroken because he has realized that he hasn't changed the world. However, he was taking the wrong approach, since such large changes result in discord and destruction, such as the displacing of the tribe. Celie, Shug, Sofia, Odessa, and Squeak have all taken care of each other, and the courses of their lives have all been dramatically affected by each other. It is possible to make a difference in this world, just by changing one person. Now that Samuel and Nettie have each other, they can start changing the world one person at a time.

Study Questions

1. How is Nettie surprised by her own appearance?
2. What do Nettie and Samuel now do for the Olinka tribe?
3. What are the signs all over Africa that a war is coming?
4. Why does Doris decide against becoming a nun?
5. What is the pseudonym of Doris Baines?
6. What pleasure is Doris willing to pay handsomely for?
7. What do people that meet Samuel and Nettie on the street in England always say?
8. What are some of the questions that the Olinka tribe always asked the missionaries?
9. What would have happened if Adam struck Tashi?
10. What does Nettie call Samuel in the postscript of her letter to Celie?

Answers

1. Nettie has become "plump and graying."

2. Nettie and Samuel do nothing now but teach the young children.

3. Roads are being built to where supplies are kept. The trees are being cut down in order to make "ships and captain's furniture." Land is being planted with "something you can't eat," and the natives are forced to work on these fields. Doris takes all of these events as signs of an impending war.

4. Doris Baines wanted nothing more than to be her own boss. If she chose to become a nun, then God would be her boss.

5. Her pen name is Jared Hunt.

6. For Doris, the pleasure of being alone is without price.

7. Passers-by always seem to notice how much Adam and Olivia look like Nettie.

8. Samuel says that the people of the tribe ask missionaries questions like: "Why don't you speak our language? Why can't you remember the old ways? Why aren't you happy in America, if everyone there drives motorcars?"

9. If Adam ever hit her, Nettie says that Tashi would put his head "through her rug loom."

10. Samuel is called Celie's brother in Nettie's letter.

Suggested Essay Topics

1. What do you think the mbeles symbolize in this novel?

2. Female circumcision as a ritual in Africa is examined more closely in a later Walker novel, *Possessing the Secret of Joy*. What ideas about this ritual are evident in this novel?

Letters 82–85

New Character:

Germaine: *a young musician*

Summary

Celie gets a call from Daisy informing her that Alphonso, her stepfather, has died. Celie is unmoved by this until she finds out that she and Nettie have inherited his house and dry goods store. Celie wants to give up the house when Shug has a better idea. They go to the house with cedar sticks and use smoke to chase "out all the evil" and make "a place for good." Celie now has a new store to sell pants.

Unfortunately, while she fixes up her home she is barraged with bad news. Shug tells her that she met a young man one night, and that she is going out on the road with him. Celie is shocked, and cannot believe her. She tells Shug that "if words could kill, I'd be in the ambulance," but Shug keeps talking, trying to make her understand that she feels old now and she needs to be with a man once again. She pleads with Celie to let her have six months for "my last fling."

While Shug is gone, Celie helps Sofia try to cure Henrietta. Celie remembers a letter from Nettie that promoted yams as a cure, but Henrietta refuses to eat them. Mr.____ comes up with some recipes that help hide the taste of yams and impresses Celie with his house, which is cleaner than ever. She knows Mr.____ is turning over a new leaf when he places a letter in her hand. This letter, however, is a telegram saying that Nettie and Samuel's ship has sunk off of Gibraltar. In light of this tragedy, Celie tries to keep sewing, but "being alive begin to seem like an awful strain" to her.

Analysis

Celie's unexpected windfall seems like a blessing. Now that a woman like Celie possesses the capital to make a real difference in the lives of other people, she should be prepared to create an international network of support. Instead, she has to endure a greater test of faith than anything she had to suffer through as the wife of Mr.____. She must somehow cope with the loss of Nettie and Shug.

Shug's revelation comes as a shock to Celie because she had really believed that Shug loved her. The sense of rejection she feels is overwhelming because she had finally become optimistic about the future and her friends. This rejection, however, is worse than anything that that Mr.____ could do to her, because she had never trusted him. Shug, for her part, still feels she needs the love of a man to make herself complete. Now that she is older, and feels less attractive, she desperately tries to have an affair with a younger man in order to show herself she is still desirable. The irony of this scene is that while Shug admires Celie for her strength and her steadfastness; Shug admits that she "is too weak a woman" to refuse the company of a man. Celie, however, feels the same kind of nothingness that she felt when she found out about Mr.____'s deception. She equates Shug's choice of Germaine as an act of ultimate betrayal. She also feels that her network of support has been destroyed. As a result, she finds that life isn't important to her anymore. She equates solitude with the abuse that she had to suffer.

Study Questions

1. How come Celie still calls Alphonso "Pa"?

2. What does Alphonso leave Daisy?

3. How many children is Daisy left with?

4. What fortune does Celie read from her fortune cookie?

5. What did Shug feel about Grady?

6. What has happened to Grady and Mary Agnes?

7. Why does Shug talk about Cuba?

8. Name a recipe that Mr.____ devises to hide the taste of yams.

9. Why does the thought of getting pregnant make Celie want to cry?

10. What supposedly happens to Nettie's ship?

Answers

1. Celie says that it is "too late to call him Alphonso."

2. Daisy is left all of Alphonso's money, along with the clothes and the car. She also takes all of the furniture from the house, saying that Alphonso bought it for her anyway.

3. Daisy has two children from Alphonso and is pregnant with a third.

4. Celie's fortune says "Because you are who you are, the future looks happy and bright."

5. Even though Grady was Shug's husband, all he seemed to think about was "women and reefer." Celie had noticed that Grady "never brought a sparkle to" Shug's eyes.

6. Grady and Mary Agnes now own a marijuana farm in Panama. Mary Agnes still sings, but they both smoke marijuana excessively. She cannot remember all the words to the songs.

7. Shug talks about having an exciting time in Cuba with Celie in order to distract her from the news that she has fallen in love with Germaine.

8. Mr.____ has the idea of mixing yams with peanut butter to hide the taste.

9. Celie is so unhappy with life because she is all alone following Shug's departure. Furthermore, she had just told Mr.____ that "men look like frogs." She is disillusioned with marriage and love between men and women, and pregnancy is a symbol of that love to her.

10. Nettie's ship was allegedly sunk by German mines.

Suggested Essay Topics

1. What do you think Daisy's fate will be? What is the significance of her character?

2. Analyze the scene in which Celie and Shug visit Alphonso's grave. Compare this scene to the scene in which they search for the graves of Celie's real parents.

Letters 86–87

New Characters:

Stanley Earl: *Eleanor Jane's husband*

Reynolds Stanley: *the baby son of Stanley Earl and Eleanor Jane*

James: *Shug Avery's son*

Summary

Nettie writes that Tashi has run away with her mother to join the mbeles. Although Nettie is upset, there is nothing more that she or her family can do in Africa. The rest of the tribe is dying out due to malaria and other diseases, as a result of the lack of yams that were once plentiful in the region. The family decides to return to America, where Nettie hopes to find Celie. Nettie cannot believe that it has been 30 years since they have last met, and she hopes that living with Mr.____ has not changed her character or her spirit. As she finishes her letter, however, she hears that Adam has left the village, presumably in search of Tashi.

Celie, meanwhile, continues to write to Nettie because she feels her sister is still alive. Shug has been traveling with Germaine around the country, longer than the six months that she asked for. She has met one of her children in Arizona, and is spending time with him. Her other children refuse to see her. Now that she is re-united with family, Shug writes Celie once a week, and Celie has accepted the fact that she loves another. Celie hopes that Shug will one day return, and even if "she want to come back dragging Germaine I'd make them both welcome or die trying."

With Shug gone, Celie spends a lot of time with Sofia and Harpo, although Henrietta is still battling sickness. Eleanor Jane's constant visits with her new baby start to become a nuisance to Sofia. Finally, Sofia tells Eleanor Jane that she is tired of the baby's interference and Eleanor Jane's presence. Eleanor breaks down because she always thought that Sofia was her friend, not understanding that Sofia was only there under threat of a jail sentence.

Celie also spends more time with Mr.____; surprisingly, Celie cannot bring herself to hate him. Since he loved Shug, the two do have something in common. Mr.____ takes advantage of this by asking all of the questions about her childhood that he never bothered to ask when he was married to her. He is shocked to learn that she was damaged by her stepfather, and admits that he used to beat her because she was not Shug. However, he feels sorry for Celie because Shug left her. He remembers how bad he felt when Shug left him.

Celie and Mr.____ act like "two old fools left over from love, keeping each other company under the stars." Celie tells him about her pants business, mentioning that what makes her pants so special is that "anybody can wear them." Mr.____ thinks only men can wear pants but then remembers how fond he used to be of sewing. Celie gives Mr.____ a needle and thread and asks him to help her sew a pocket together. She notices that Mr.____ "ain't Shug, but he begin to be somebody I can talk to."

Analysis

Samuel and Nettie's world has dissolved almost completely, and the illusion under which they have lived has vanished as well. The tragedy of the Olinka tribe has caused Samuel and Nettie to decide that it is time for them to leave Africa. Although they valiantly struggled against the forces of progress, the Olinka are ultimately at fault for their own destruction; their self-centeredness doomed them to be unprepared for such a disaster. Nettie and Samuel's union, however, has prepared them for their next struggle. They have come to the same conclusion about the nature of God that Shug had extolled; God is a free spirit rather than an object to them, and this thinking frees them to find and worship God in all things.

Unfortunately, another rift occurs in the family with the disappearance of Tashi. Tashi is in the center of two conflicting philosophies—the way of the Olinka and of the missionaries. Her shame comes from feeling the need to be subjected to the scarring and the circumcision. Tashi was always an independent girl, and was one of the first girls to enter the Olinka school. To subject herself to this ritual seems to be a sign of weakness. While clothes have always been symbols of protection, Tashi has allowed herself to be cut on her bare skin, implying her new vulnerability. She reacts to

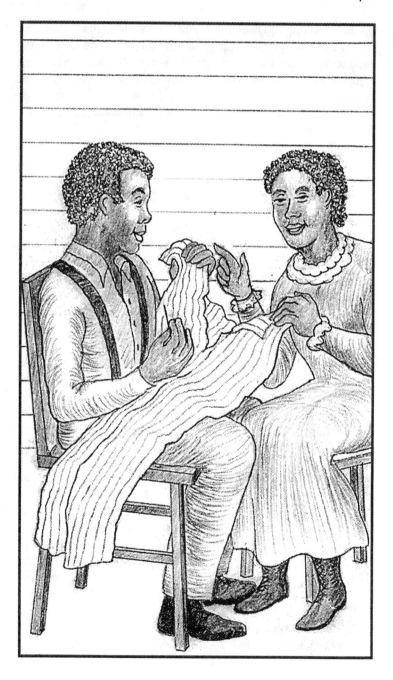

this vulnerability by leaving the village, which has already lost the roofleaf, the quilts that they loved to make, and any other object that might protect and comfort her. With Adam's rejection, she feels that she has lost the person who loves her, and so nothing is left. Adam quickly tries to find her in order to correct his hasty judgment and prove to Tashi that she still does have someone who will support and love her.

Meanwhile, Sofia finally shows Eleanor Jane that she does not want to support her. Eleanor Jane is a weak girl who always needs someone to compliment her and tell her how wonderful her life is. However, everyone else who has lived a lie in this novel eventually faced the truth. The initial brutal honesty is needed so that a new, stronger relationship can be built, e.g., Celie to Mr._____, Nettie to Corrine, Samuel to himself, and so on. Sofia had always lashed out at people who tried to control her, until doing that got her arrested. She was forced to support the mayor's family, but Eleanor Jane misinterpreted this false support as love. Her crime, however, is using this support instead of feeling confident in herself. After Sofia tells her that she doesn't like her baby, Eleanor Jane tries to make her feel guilty by projecting her own feelings onto Sofia:

> You just don't like him cause he look like daddy,
> say Miss Eleanor Jane.
> You don't like him cause he look like daddy, say
> Sofia. I don't feel nothing about him at all...

Sofia has finally asserted herself in hopes of getting back her strong family, which had always supported her. Now, the key to her family's strength lies in Henrietta, the youngest child, to whom everyone feels closely connected. Sofia strengthens her connection to Henrietta by cutting away the weaker ones, the connections she never would have chosen to make on her own.

After numerous disappointments, Celie has managed to put her life back together. She has also become more inclusive in her network of support. When Shug took a lover, Celie felt not only rejected but betrayed due to her understandable hatred of men. This caused Celie to reject Shug's friendship completely and drive her away from her life. The void that Shug leaves in Celie's life makes Celie reconsider and, like Adam, she understands that the love of another person means more to her than any disappointment she might feel. Once she is willing to accept everybody and the decisions that are made by these people, she again gains strength. Her new relationship with Mr.____ is the result of this new strength; she even teaches him to sew, proving that her love is great enough to reach people that seemed the least likely to protect another human being.

Study Questions

1. Why is Samuel pretty confident that his family will not get malaria, even though there is an epidemic in the village?

2. What sort of church does Nettie and Samuel hope to found in America?

3. Why do the Olinka have "shallow" relationships with the missionaries?

4. Name some of the places that Shug and Germaine visit.

5. What does Eleanor Jane do to Sofia that is more annoying than complaining about her problems?

6. According to Stanley Earl, why do white folks "turn out so well"?

7. How does Sofia feel about little Reynolds Stanley Earl?

8. When did Shug's parents die?

9. What does Mr.____ mean when he says "If a mule could tell folks how it's treated, it would"?

10. How do the Olinka interpret the identity of the biblical Adam?

Answers

1. Nettie, Samuel, Adam, and Olivia have all survived bouts with malaria.

2. Nettie wants to start a church "in which each person's spirit is encouraged to seek God directly."

3. The Olinka know that eventually the missionaries will leave, making a relationship pointless.

4. Celie receives letters from Shug in New York, California, Arizona, and Panama, where she and Germaine were visiting Grady and Squeak.

5. Eleanor Jane starts to bother Sofia whenever anything good happens, insisting that Sofia say nice things about her husband and son.

6. White folks turn out well because "everybody round here raised by colored."

7. Sofia doesn't really care about Eleanor Jane's baby one way or the other, as long as he could keep quiet more often.

8. Shug's parents had died nine or ten years ago.

9. Mr.____ is no longer mad that Celie told Shug how he treated her, because the bigger crime was treating her that way in the first place. A work animal would complain about the injustice if it could speak, and Celie was treated like an animal, so it was only natural that she complain.

10. According to Olinka legend, every person that came before Adam was black. But then, women started to give birth to "colorless" babies, for some unknown reason. At first, these babies were killed, but they kept being born. Adam is the first white baby that wasn't killed.

Suggested Essay Topics

1. How does Sofia's relationship with Eleanor Jane compare with her relationship with Miss Millie? Who had the upper hand in each relationship? Discuss and compare them.

2. Discuss the significance of yams in this section. To what themes are they related?

Letters 88–90

Summary

Nettie writes happily that Adam and Tashi have returned. While Adam and Tashi were in the forest, they uncovered a huge hidden city full of displaced members of different tribes. When they return, Adam asks Tashi to marry him, but she refuses. Tashi is afraid that with her scars she will be looked upon as a savage in America and Adam will eventually become ashamed of her. Adam promises her that he will always be with her, and proves this by having his face scarred in the same manner. Tashi and Adam are married by Samuel, and they immediately set out for home.

While Celie waits for Nettie to come home, she sets up her store and employs Sofia as a clerk. Harpo takes care of the children. He gets some extra help from Eleanor Jane, who found out why Sofia was her maid and feels the need to make amends. Mr.____ asks Celie to marry him again, and Celie offers to be his friend instead. Just when Celie knows she "can live content without Shug," she gets a letter from Shug which says that she is coming back. Celie guesses that to be content on one's own is "the lesson I suppose to learn."

One day, while Shug, Albert, and Celie are sitting on the porch, they see a car in the distance. The car pulls up to their driveway and Nettie, Samuel, Olivia, Adam, and Tashi get out and walk up to the porch. Celie and Nettie fall into each other's arms and cry.

The last scene is at the family reunion, which always takes place on the Fourth of July. It is a gigantic barbecue, with everyone laughing and enjoying each other's company. Celie looks at everyone and marvels that she is actually reunited with her sister. Even though it has been 30 years since she has last seen her and she is an old woman, she thinks "this is the youngest [I] ever felt."

Analysis

All of the conflicts in this novel are resolved in the final section. Even though Nettie and Samuel plan to leave Africa after the destruction of the Olinka tribe, Adam and Tashi discover a grand, unified tribe hidden in a canyon. This society is almost a utopia,

or perfect society, in which black men and women from all over Africa have worked together for a common cause. The missionaries leave Africa with the suggestion that some people will not suffer from the same lack of perspective that doomed the Olinka tribe. Adam scars his cheeks as a symbol to Tashi. He, too, is "marked" and will suffer from the same isolation that Tashi would feel in America. However, they will always be together, no matter what happens in America.

Before Celie and Shug can be reunited, Celie learns to like living even though Shug is not there. Once she does this, Celie is almost immediately rewarded with Shug's return. This was the last thing she had to learn about herself. Once she truly accepts herself, she can continue to supply the whole world with love and protection. In the final scene, all the women who have loved and protected each other come to the same place to enjoy each other. Even though certain people might go their separate ways, Celie has always been there for every woman during a crisis, and she will always be with them. Even though she is old, her youthful spirit has transcended age. The novel ends with her feeling the youngest she has ever felt. After she spent her entire life suffering, Celie has learned to love and be loved, and will spend the rest of her life loving and being loved.

Study Questions

1. How long were Adam and Tashi gone?

2. What would Tashi still have if Adam deserted her?

3. What happens when Sofia is called "auntie" by a white man?

4. What was the only thing Albert ever wanted in life?

5. Why does Albert think we are here on this earth?

6. What has happened to Germaine?

7. Will Shug ever sing again?

8. Why did Mary Agnes leave Grady?

9. What do people like to eat in Africa, according to Tashi?

10. Why does Celie feel a little peculiar around the children?

Answers

1. Adam and Tashi were gone for two and a half months.

2. Even if Adam deserted her, Tashi would still have Olivia. Olivia promises she will always be Tashi's sister.

3. Sofia asks him which colored man married his mother's sister.

4. The only thing that Albert wanted in life was Shug Avery.

5. Albert decides that people are here "to wonder," and "in wondering bout the big things...you learn bout the little ones."

6. Germaine went off to college after his split with Shug.

7. Shug contemplates retirement, although she would still sing one or two nights at Harpo's.

8. Mary Agnes was tired of being stoned all the time, and Grady was "no good influence for no child." She now lives in Memphis, with her mother and Suzie Q.

9. Tashi says that Africans love to eat barbecue.

10. The children seem to think that all of the older people "don't know much what going on." But Celie knows better.

Suggested Essay Topics

1. Is the ending of this novel "closed"? Is there anything more the reader wishes to know about Celie and Nettie?

2. What is the significance of the Fourth of July in this novel?

Sample Analytical Paper Topics

Topic #1

Follow the development of clothes as symbols in *The Color Purple* and explain how clothes become symbols of protection.

Outline

I. Thesis Statement: *In* The Color Purple, *characters who wish to protect others from harm make clothes for them. Clothes become a symbol of protection because the making of clothes is an act of support from one to another.*

II. Early examples of this symbol

    A. Celie dresses up to try to protect Nettie from Alphonso

    B. Corrine's dress for Olivia

    C. These symbols do not help Celie

III. Those that help Celie

    A. Kate's wish to make a dress

    B. Shug

        1. Donates a dress for Celie's quilt

        2. Gives Celie the idea for pants

IV. Celie as protector

    A. Sews pants for herself

    B.   For Sofia

    C.   For Nettie

    D.   For everyone

Topic #2

Use examples from the text in which the setting is either inside or near a church. Compare scenes with churches to illustrate the theme of God in *The Color Purple.*

Outline

I.   Thesis Statement: *The church is used as a symbol for God in* The Color Purple. *Early in the text, violence and injustice occur near churches in order to illustrate the inequity with which women are treated in so-called "God-fearing" towns.*

II.   Victims of church

    A.   Annie Julia is killed near a church

    B.   Celie is slapped after coming home from church

III. The ideal of God

    A.   Celie's God (stereotype)

    B.   Shug's God

IV. God and church

    A.   Celie's God is found in the town church

        1.   The people of that church have never been kind to Celie

    B.   God without church

    C.   God is found in nature

Topic #3

Compare Celie, Sofia, and Squeak as they fight the suppression that follows them throughout their lives.

Outline

I.   Thesis Statement: *How the women deal with oppression in* The Color Purple *differs, but Celie, Sofia and Squeak all eventually become self-determining women.*

II.   Squeak

   A.   The weakest of the three

   B.   Draws inspiration from other women

      1.   Celie

      2.   Shug

      3.   Sofia

   C.   Becomes sidetracked with Grady, but eventually breaks away

III. Sofia

   A.   Has the strongest character to begin with

      1.   Easily defeats Harpo

   B.   Becomes weak once in jail

   C.   Oppressed first by Miss Millie, then by Eleanor Jane

      1.   Eventually asserts herself to Eleanor Jane

IV.   Celie

   A.   The most heroic transformation

   B.   Draws inspiration

      1.   Sofia

      2.   Shug

   C.   Becomes inspiration to other women

SECTION FOUR

Bibliography

Walker, Alice. *The Color Purple.* New York: Simon & Schuster, Inc., 1982.

Winchell, Donna Haisty. *Alice Walker.* New York: Twayne Publishers, 1992.